Visa Versa

Visa Versa

◆

Black men suffer in the dating game too!

Christopher Darrick Odom

iUniverse, Inc.
New York Lincoln Shanghai

Visa Versa
Black men suffer in the dating game too!

iUniverse books may be ordered through booksellers or by contacting:

iUniverse
2021 Pine Lake Road, Suite 100
Lincoln, NE 68512
www.iuniverse.com
1-800-Authors (1-800-288-4677)

ISBN-13: 978-0-595-40351-6 (pbk)
ISBN-13: 978-0-595-84726-6 (ebk)
ISBN-10: 0-595-40351-4 (pbk)
ISBN-10: 0-595-84726-9 (ebk)

Printed in the United States of America

This book is dedicated to three Ladies in my life that I will never forget.

Marcia Laura Jumper (My first Love)

Megan Marie Bowes (My last Love)

Teresa Lanette Billingsley (The one I was dumb to let go)

Contents

PREFACE

This book is a journey of a Black man seeking a partner to share live with. He is an educated professional who finds himself alone and lonely. You as the reader follow along with him as he attempts to find a "**good**" woman. He suffers from many taboos and attacks upon his character for being a Black man. He hears how "**bad**" Black men are and he is challenged to overcome these myths.

With him, you will feel, as he suffers through friends setting him up, his dating services experiences, he tries personal ads and even the church, only to find that the same heartaches, pain and suffering are endured by Black men as Black women. The stories will cause you to think, laugh and cry as you journey with our SBM seeking a "good" SBF.

Alone with stories of his experiences there are reflection in verse on his suffering, observations and personal challenges. The last story will just make you cry.

INTRODUCTION

I am a Proud Black man from the United States. Born and raised here. But as a **Proud Black Man** I find it difficult to just say that. I also see that weather here in the states or Jamaica, Haiti, Africa, or South America we Black men appear to evoke the same impression.

We are worthless, abusive, ill responsible, seed spreading, HIV spreading, dangerous, womanizing, child raping, jail jumping, down low and out right low down animals. I am always trying to fight this stigma but it seems to deaf ears and blind eyes. As a Proud Black Man I want the world to know that we can and are people of feelings, emotions, vibrancy and eminence, but no matter what I am always "The Black Man." When I walk into a room filled with Tuxedo wearing men of all nationalities, I will be, "The Black Man." When I walk down the street, white women grasp their purse and see, "The Black Man." When I walk pass a person sitting in their car I hear the doors lock because they see, "The Black Man." I, "The Black Man," will always be thought of as that, abusive, ill responsible, seed spreading, HIV spreading, dangerous, womanizing, child raping, jail jumping, down low and out right low down animals

I am a failure to my Queens; I have communicated with and talked to so many women that I am rather tired and ready to settle down alone. After many attempts to find a Black woman to share my life with, I suffered a horrific marriage with a gold digging debasing woman. I have chased after white women to find they only wanted to dance with my anaconda and weren't interested in me as a partner. I have chased after Asian women to find that my color is something they detest but will tolerate if I can show them a good time. I have been chased by women much younger than I only to see they want my wallet and chased by older women to find they want to control the relationship. Failing to discover true commitment I resolve to be alone. My lovely dog Iman comes to me and sticks her head between my legs and looks up at me. She turns around and offers her boodie to me to smack. What more can a man want. Funny though it seems, the real joke is that I am a joke.

This Book is to show my Queen how troublesome it is for even us, The Black Man, in our search to find a Queen to share life with. We need to exhale just as much at Terry McMillan's 1992 novel wrote about regarding Black ladies. My ladies give just as much trouble to us as we are reported to be given to them in all the movies, news and churches.

The stories are all true even though the names are changed. My quest starts when I was in my twenties continuing into my late thirties. Today I still am alone and I plan to stay that way. It may sound arrogant to say but I am the type of Black man that ends up with a white woman in America. Professional, educated, and upwardly mobile Black men tend to marry white women. I only wanted a Black lady to be the Queen of my world and the mother of my future.

I've been told to lower my standards because the world is changing and I must accept the change. I am the first advocate of change but not all change is good. I am embarrassed to walk down the street as I see my image disgrace the name of manhood. I see me raping young girls in Africa because I need to fill my primal need. I am disgusted to see me destroy the paradise I have devastated in Haiti. I allow wealth to corrupt my dignity as I make films that portray me as a thug, criminal, and giving no positive reinforcement. Standards must be lowered as the world changes because the money is good. Yet with all the wealth I still have communities which I can not move into. There are still countries that don't want me to visit let lone live. Women still tremble in fear as I walk pass. Other men still think of me as a criminal. To lower my standards for times a changing yet we still are worthless, abusive, ill responsible, seed spreading, HIV spreading, dangerous, womanizing, child raping, jail jumping, down low and out right low down animals in the viewpoint of the world.

I am not that and there are many like me. I would guess to say more like me than like that. The problem is that my Queens can only see them and not me. Furthermore there are a great deal of worthless, abusive, ill responsible, leg spreading, HIV spreading, dangerous, male debasing, manhood raping, jail jumping, down low and out right low down animals that are Black ladies.

REFLECTIONS
LET ME LOVE YOU

You process strength unparalleled to anyone or anything. Just look at what you have to endure. From our coronation onto this great land of pain, suffering, discernment, and disgrace, you have had to stand strong, and you managed to preserve your pride and foundation.

From the beginning, you had to put up with the defilement of your body and soul. Striped from your home, chained and quartered as property, you became a bed warmer to an oppressive salacious heathen, yet you were exclaimed as uncivilized. You had to capitulate to beatings, scores of rapes, and forced to perform disgusting acts by those who claimed to be civilized.

You had to in turn watch as the oppressive heathen humiliate your man by beating and castrating him. You must have been brimming with anguish to see your strong man reduced to an inconsequential phantasm of a man.

You were told/forced to bear children by whoever the oppressor chose. You were put to work in the fields and beaten while carrying your children. You were a private harlot to the oppressor, while he treated his women as a queen, and when you carried his child, you got no better treatment.

You cried and pleaded while your children were taken from you to be sold. You were used as a breeding mechanism as if you had not any feelings or prudence. The rape of your body produced a brood of descendants unintentionally designed to further ostracize the family unit, also the race.

From this degradation, your man lost his self-respect and turned from you. You had to suffer from his lost pride, you also endured the attitude he embraced, that he was unable to retrieve his pride back. Although you continue to concentrate your efforts toward helping your man capturing back his dignity, he punctures your efforts.

You have to live with the knowing that your man beats you, humiliates you, rapes you, and eventually leaves you in order to prove to himself, he is a man. His apathetic reasoning causes him to be no better than the oppressor.

You now find yourself raising you children alone. You are hailed as a lazy welfare whores. You carry the responsibility of the future of your community on your back without any accolades. What you get in return is seeing your men running around with the oppressor's woman, putting them on pedestals while criticizing you.

It is hard to believe I am telling the story of women whores' history has the destiny to be queen. From Cleopatra to Nefretiri, African women have been the model of beauty.

Queens you are to me. I know how you have suffered. I love you for your suffering. I only want to put your pain to rest. I am born of you, and it gives me great pride to know I come from such beauty, strength, and tenacity. I have, however, a problem with you allowing me to love you.

Decades of abuse by all classes of human essence have branded much bitterness in you. Continued castration of your feminine dignity has carved multitudinous scars in your hart. Ostracize by those you, most care for has cemented your love in an impenetrate crypt.

You were extorted into the position of power you find yourself within. You did not ask to watch as your man was torn down to a shell. You did not request your body to be defiled. You had no wishes to cause the pollution of your race from the seed of the oppressor. Your ego did not hunger for the envy of your oppressors' woman. You were elevated to that position of power by circumstance.

I fully understand your need to catacomb your venerability. As I search for your love, I experience the remains of what my counterparts abandoned after they have ravaged you. With all you have had to put up with through out the ages, the proud, beautiful and dynamic lady you are, you still find yourself venerable to continual anguish. That which you quest for most, seems to elude you by an overwhelming scale. You covet and warrant your true destiny, to be queen.

I love you and want you to be queen of my world, yet I suffer unending wounds from your sword of self-preservation. With great appreciation of your need to protect yourself from the legacy my counterparts have established, I graciously yield myself to your defense. Please, I ask of you, do not thrust your sword so deep. I am a man who appreciates you. I am not after your body to use as a pleasure palace. My wishes are not to be conqueror over you, nor do I wish to abandon you in arduous moments.

I do not wish to look to any other race for a mate. Your beauty is unmatched and envied by all others. Your strength and dedication is an admirable quality of which I find palatable. I have only the desire to give all my strength to you so you can relax from your long struggle. I want to turn your dreams to reality. You need not to suffer any more, just let me carry your cross. I know you have just reason to question my intentions; however, I am not just another Brother out to get what he can. I want to give to you your destiny. How long will it take for you to realize I mean what I am declaring? I will gladly take all the stabs. I will do whatever it takes to prove to you I want to make you queen.

My thoughts are not of a casual nature. My feelings are strong and I express them in genuine emotions of respect, compassion and love for my Black women.

CHAPTER ONE
BRENDA

Brenda was a classic beauty. She was tall and slender. She had deep rich penetrating brown eyes. The first time I saw her I almost melted from her beauty. She had a soft yet determined voice. Everything about her was perfection. There was only one major problem with her. I was interviewing her for a job.

At first, the conversation was very businesslike. I could tell that not only was she knock dead gorgeous, she was an extremely intelligent lady as well. She had drive, self-motivation, and goals. She was determined to be successful. I could tell she was going to be a success someday.

Her eyes were captivating. As I sat there interviewing her I couldn't help but to fall for her. I found myself in a very arduous position. Here sitting across from me is the most attractive lady that has crossed my path in years. The man-child in me wanted to tell her what I felt. I wanted to tell her she was a very attractive lady, with a stimulating intellect. I wanted to tell her I wanted to be the man in her life.

The professional in me couldn't help to see a person that could be an outstanding asset for my company. As it is typical for me the professional side of me took precedence over the man in me, as well as it should have been.

I was trying to build a strong cohesive team the make my unit among the best in the company. I worked for a major retailer. My particular unit was located with a Black community. The feeling of the powers that be, was, it was a location that was not going to amount to much of anything purely because of the neighborhood.

I was placed in that unit solely because of the color of my skin. The feeling was that since it was a "Black Store," It would be best run by a Black manager. The mind set behind this train of thought was, that Blacks are animalistic thieves and if they were gong to do business in that community, why waste a valuable white manager in a unit that could only loose money.

From the time I first stepped onto the premises I was bombarded with racial remarks and innuendoes by the White men who called themselves my boss. I constantly herd the words, inner city store, and theft mentioned together on a daily basis. With this in mind I knew I had to develop a team that would make fool of the White ignorance I was encountering.

All of this was racing through my mind as I sat across from this Nubian goddess. She surely had intelligence. She was tough; my interviewing practices are not for the meager or insecure. Still I had to ask myself was she what I needed to strengthen my team? Was my mind stimulated by her as a potential associate, or was my interest in her primal?

I have always been accused of being married to my work. The fact that Brenda was not only attractive and alluring; she also displayed a strong sense of work ethic, drive, and strength, caused me to want her more. My mind began to race. I had to be professional. I couldn't let on how I felt about her.

I offered her a position with another department. This was extremely crazy on my part because I knew she would be great for my department. The only reason I did such a stupid thing was so I would not be her manager. This would give me the opportunity to let my feeling be known without compromising my professionalism. She said no. My department was where she wanted to be.

Not to be out done I checked her credentials and saw where she lived was closer to another location. I informed her that I could get her in at that location, being that it was closer to home. I thought this would work. At a different location, I could visit her and with any luck, I could then develop a relationship with her.

Again, she said no, she stated, she had heard of my reputation and wanted to work at my location. She was good; I have to give her that. Not only beautiful, strong, intelligent, but she knew what she wanted and was determined to get it.

Finally, I gave in. My hart was beating strong for her, and I couldn't persuade her to go somewhere else so I could tell her of my desires. Not only were my desires taking my mind off work, they were about to let me loose an outstanding asset for my department. When I began to realize this fact, I hired her right away.

The first few months went smoothly with Brenda. We had a very businesslike relationship. At first, I thought I had made a mistake. She didn't seem to catch on to what I expected of her. My first thought was that I was putting too much pressure on her. Somehow, I wanted her to be the best associate I had. I of course was not aware of the pressure. It was not until she told me I wasn't being fair, that I realized what I was doing.

Back in my dark little mind, I was trying to prove to myself that I'd hired her not because of her beauty, or because of my attraction for her, but because of her great expertise. I wanted, no needed her to be my best associate. Only then could I justify in my mind that I hired her for purely business sake.

It wasn't until one of my one-on-one training sessions that she advised me of my playing favorites, and that she was not one of my favorites. Little did she know I favored her over them all! I wanted to say to her, "you silly lady, I love everything about you. I want to sweep you up and take you away with me!" Thank goodness, I kept my sense.

I realized my admiration for her had caused me to be harder on her. When I decided to let my feelings for her take a back burner, I was able to treat her as a regular employee. The following months proved to be profitable for the company and successful for our department.

In those months, I began to get to know Brenda better, not just as an employee but also as a person. I would see hoards of men come to see her. I would feel a great sense of loss and jealousy but I would not allow myself to cross the line of employer and employee. She would at times during training sessions, offer me some tidbits of her life and relationships.

She would tell me stories of disappointment, despair, and fear from all the many men that would cross her path. We turned into very good friends, but only on job friends. Each day my admiration for her grew. She was bright, strong, very demanding, and beautiful. Many a times I wanted to throw away my professional ethics, go up to her, sweep her off her feet, and carry her off.

Months had gone by when unexpectedly a bizarre yet welcome episode took place. One of my employees, one of which I did think of as my favorite, took it upon herself along with one other employee to set up a blind date for me. Betty and Andre came to me and explained they had a lady they want me to meet.

They both acted very suspicious. We were a close team and all, but I felt there was something going on. I asked why they would want to set me up. Their response was that I worked too hard and I needed to find someone to make me happy. Flattered I said I would meet their friend. We arranged to go to dinner after work.

After work, we met in the employee parking lot. To my surprise, there was Brenda. My hart almost drooped to the ground. Betty and Andre were laughing as they saw the look in my face. Betty stopped laughing for a moment to get serious.

"You know you like Brenda, and I know Brenda likes you. You two have been working much too hard to try not to show it, but everyone can see you two like each other. Andre and I decided to put you together. After all you both are alike and both of you need and deserve someone nice."

As Betty went on telling us all about ourselves in a way, only Betty could. I stood there looking at Brenda in a state of shock.

Brenda looked at me as if she was just as much embarrassed and surprised as I. I just stood there staring into Brenda's beautiful eyes while Betty went on and on about how we both work too much, and how pitiful we were to allow a job to stand in the way of our happiness.

When Betty stopped talking and stated we better get on to dinner, several emotions went through me. First, I was mad for them to do this to us. Then I felt happy because this was after all what I wanted. Then a great sense of fear crossed over me that I could not shake. As we crowded in the car to make our dinner reservations, I could not speak from fear. Oddly enough, Brenda didn't say a word either.

Dinner was awkward but the conversation was mostly about work and small talk about world events. Brenda and I spent most of the time looking at each other. I didn't know what she was thinking. I was thinking about all the things I have wanted to say to her but fear was overwhelming me.

Betty and Andre had another trick up their sleeves. They excused themselves to sit at the bar, leaving Brenda and me there alone to talk. There I was sitting across from the lady of my dreams and I scared to death. At first we laughed and talked about how crazy both Andre and Betty were to do such a thing.

When we did get around to talking about us I realized Brenda had the same feelings I did. She was interested in me but had a hard time dealing with the conflict of us being coworkers. More than that, she was concerned that I was her boss. As I sat there hearing her talk about professional ethics, and conduct in the work place, I knew this was the lady for me. We were two of a kind.

During the course of our conversation, I fell in love with Brenda. I wanted her in my life and was willing to give it a shot. Still I was afraid. I have never dated an employee nor had I had any feeling to do so in the past. I told this to Brenda and informed her that it may be awkward for me and for her, but if she thought she could separate her professional life from her personal life, and if I could, it would be worth a try.

The next day it was business as usual. After confessing our feeling for each other, it was clear we still were afraid to move on our feelings. We did not mention the previous night at all. We both acted as if we knew a great secret. All we did was smile at each other and went about doing our jobs. This went on for a week until Betty jumped in and kept badgering me to ask Brenda out for a date. I found out latter Andre was working on Brenda to make a move.

My fear was too great. I even went to a manager of another department who was a friend and asked if he had dated an employee of his. He said he had and not to worry about it because there wasn't any company rule against it as long as the lady was interested.

To be honest my fear was not from the repercussions that may come from my job for violating a company policy. I was more afraid of Brenda. I wondered if I deserved her. She was extremely attractive. She was smart, demanding, professional and sexy. I wondered if I were good enough for her. I was using the job to support my insecurities. Still after a week of pretending dinner had not happened, I thought I should at lease try to overcome my fears and see if Brenda and I could become a couple.

Our first date went very well. We laughed and enjoyed each other. We talked about past relationships, politics, religion, and expectations. We talked extensively about the condition of Black relationships. That is when I learned that Brenda had a difficult time with many of my Black brothers.

She went on about how most Black men tend to be intimidated by her looks. Either they felt she was too good for them and all they want to do was get her in bed to make them feel good, or they put her down in order for her to feel less worthy. She questioned why most of them lie about having children, wives, or girlfriends. I could tell she had been hurt by my Black brothers, yet I had seen her determination, her professionalism and knew she was not going to let her bad luck in love tear her down. I admired her for this.

After the date, I walked her to her car and said good-by. I didn't try to kiss her good-by because I didn't want her to think I was after anything else. Besides I am an old fashion guy and do not attack a lady. I want to show my respect and build a friendship first. This I found out latter was my first mistake.

The next few dates we had were wonderful. We enjoyed each other's, company. We were able to talk about anything. We debated, laughed, and questioned. We were becoming very good friends. I was falling in love with Brenda. She was in my every thought. I knew I had found the lady of my dreams. I had to pinch myself every day to make sure I wasn't dreaming.

It wasn't long when I started noticing Brenda was still receiving many male visitors at work. I brushed it off, as it was dew to her gorgeous looks. I had not felt any need to get jealous. Then one night out of the blue Brenda told me I was too good for her. She further stated we should see other people.

I asked her what was wrong. She brought up our first date. She stated that when I didn't try to kiss her goodnight she felt I was not interested in her. She went on to say that since I have not tried to make love to her, she thought I was gay. Then she had to nerve to ask me if I were gay.

I became furious. The first thought in my mind was to take her home and screw her brains out. Then I calmed down realizing that would prove nothing. How could we have had such a wonderful time together and she thinks this? All this time, I am thinking we were building a strong relationship, and she was looking for me to be as much an animal as other men in her life.

I asked her if she wanted me to like her for what she had between her legs or did she want me to like her for what she was. I told her I had great respect for her and chose not to treat her as a slut for me to conquest. I thought we were going to build a future together and I thought she deserved to be treated with loving reverence.

I reminded her of the many stories she told me of men who treated her like trash for their own satisfaction. I tried t explained that I wanted our relationship to be different. When I took her home I was so full of indignation I could barley walk her to the door.

On my drive home, I was filled with anger, sorrow, and hurt that a profusion of thoughts flew through my mind. How could she say I was too good for her? Because I don't rape her? Because I don't beat her? Because I think her exterior beautiful extends deeper that the eye can see? By the time I got home, I had decided not to see her again outside work.

By the next morning, I had lost my anger. I realized being a beautiful Black lady was a curse for Brenda. The fact that she was bright, independent, and determined beautiful Black lady, made her curse more intense. When I look at the history of my Black male counterparts, I can understand to a degree where she was coming from.

When love them and leave them with a baby appears to be status quo. When beat them and tare them down is a method of control. When love as many as you can is their motto. I can understand why Brenda didn't understand where I was coming from. After all, I was a Black man. What made me different? Unless I was gay, she must have felt, I should act the same. It is a sad state of affairs we have within our relationships. We have to fight the world and while immerse in that battle, we have to battle each other.

By the time I got to work, I wanted to sweep her up and tell her I was different. I wanted to tell her I loved her for the person I have gotten to know. In addition, if or when we got together it will be for the right reasons. Not because it is expected.

Brenda must have been doing some hard thinking herself. Before I could say anything to her, she came to me and apologized for her actions. We talked a while, but because we were at work, we decided to put it all behind us and go forward. It wasn't long after that I moved on and wasn't her boss anymore. Still we saw each other and had a wonderful time.

I still didn't make love to her, not because I didn't want to. I was afraid that if I did I would loose her. By making love to her, I would prove to be the same as those other men in her life. I wasn't trying to sit on some kind of high horse, I loved Brenda and wanted her to feel she deserved better than she had received.

Just as everything was going good, she did it again. Brenda started talking about other men at the most inopportune times. Telling me of the many men that ask her out, she would make comments about how she wanted to move up into management herself and really had little time for anyone. She talked of moving out of state.

Now I willing to take some abuse to show my love but even I have limits. All I was trying to accomplish was to love Brenda. I didn't want of hurt her, yet it seemed to me she was trying to hurt me. Was my respect for her that hard to understand? Often times when I look back at those days I wish I had treated her a little like she expected me to.

I remember one incident at her apartment. I had gone over to spend time with her. We talked for hours and I had a good time. When it was time for me to go, she reached out to me and screamed for me not to go. I could have taken that moment to sleep with her. I knew that is what she was hoping I would do. Instead, I stayed and we talked for hours more. I wonder what would have happened if I had made love to her?

Still when she started talking about those other men and talking about leaving town, I knew I couldn't take much more. She never once said she didn't want to see me anymore. I never had to chase after her for attention. She was always there for me and I for her. Somehow, for some reason she always kept me at bay.

She finally got into the management program at work, as I knew she would. I was going through a training program myself where I was now located. We saw very little of each other during that time. We kept in contact but I missed her. I somehow felt this was the end of us, and sure enough, I was right.

One day I got a call from her on my answering machine at home. It was her leaving me a phone number where she could be reached. I realized that the area code was out of town. My hart fell to the floor. When I decided to call her back, Brenda told me she would be moving to another town through her new promotion. She told me that she will be back in town to collect her things and will be throwing a going away party.

On the day of Brenda's party, I was so hurt that I did not go. It would be extremely hard for me to say good-by to the lady of my dreams. We had invested much time in developing a relationship and yet simultaneously we exhausted much energy keeping each other at bay.

The next day while I was at work Brenda came to visit me. She didn't want to leave without saying good-by. I hate good-by's, even more so, I hated saying good-by to a lady I love. When I looked up and saw her standing there I nearly fell apart. Holding myself together I looked into her deep penetrating eyes for the last time. We said our good-by's and that was the last time I heard from Brenda.

REFLECTIONS
PLEASE OPEN THE DOOR

Damn you for how you make me feel
You make me prove myself in order to gain your attentions
I must plead to gain your affections
You persecute me as if I were the catalyst of your suffering
All I want to do is show you the love I have to give
What I receive in return is your emotions in foreclosure

Damn you for doing what you do to me
I sometimes feel like grabbing you and palpitating you with my love
Other times I just want to say to hell with you
I have looked to the other race thinking they may offer less stress
Then I hate you more for causing me to take that look

You are a proud black lady, I love you for that
You are a strong and willful lady, that, I love just as much
You have suffered in monumental proportions, this I know
You doubt my sincerity; I can understand where that comes from

Damn-it-all, I love you, just allow me the chance to show it
I'm willing to suffer through all your test and penance
All I ask is for you to create a modest door in your wall
let me in, if not for just a moment
I want to relinquish all my love to you and make you happy

REFLECTIONS
FOR FEAR WE MAY FIND
WHAT WE COVET

Your distance frightens me
    For I want you so near
        Yet, I also stand far
I feel we both want the same
    We are afraid to call it by name
Our fears of tomorrow keep us apart
    We each need to take one small step forward
        Inch by inch we can bridge this gap of fear
I feel we both are running from it
    For fear, we may find what we covet

CHAPTER TWO
HALLOW BE THY NAME

My story must begin with my upbringing. When I was five years old, my father died in a factory fire. My mother was a dumb old' country girl left with two little children to rise. They had moved to the "Big City" from a very depressed south back in the early fifties.

It was their intentions to get away from family and conditions that gave them much grief. They had experienced racial hostilities and family constrictions that made their life hell. The city did not provide such a better life as they hoped, but it gave them a chance to do something different. Now after only seven years of marriage my mother was left to raise two children without any other family to help her.

To call my mother a "dumb old' country girl" would be accurate to a small point. She was from the country that much was true. She was not too swift in the ways of the world, that too was true, but she was not dumb. My mother could have easily taken to government assistance. She didn't.

She sold everything she could to bury my father. This was hard enough because she had very little to start with. She also made sure my father received a proper burial in his hometown. After she accomplished this momentous task, she decided to make a living for her family. She took two jobs in order for her children to have the proper clothes and have three square meals a day.

Soon as she thought she was stable enough she went back to school. My mother wasn't sure if she had finished high school or not. You see back where she had grown up only privileged children went to school in a regular fashion. She had to stay home and work in the fields or clean house. Chores took precedence over school in her time. Therefore, she went to school when times allowed.

Momma did remember going to high school but could not remember graduating. Rather than looking back Momma chose to start her education with high school. Looking back was one thing I never saw my Momma do in all the years I've known her. That was one strong and determined little Black lady. She worked, went to school and took very good care of her children, all without any help from anyone else.

Education was, and still is Momma's magnificent force. Not only would she learn from her instructors, she would bring home her knowledge and feed it to my sister and myself along with our meals. She would read her lessons to us and make us read them as well. She was a strong taskmaster regarding our education. She made us learn new words every week. She made our small minds understand the things she was learning in school.

High School led to Junior College. Junior College led to universities. Diplomas let to Degrees. Every step of the way Momma brought us with her, teaching us, motivating us, and developing us. I'm getting ahead of myself. Momma continued her education while all the time working, sometimes two job at a time. She never allowed her drives get in way of her raising her children.

My sister and I were not starving from her love. We did many tings together. Our childhood was as plentiful as if Momma was always around. She was a teacher but she was a mother as well. Always going forward, she took us to zoos, parks, concerts. I remember when she took us to see the Jackson Five. We were all excited to see them perform. This was when they first went out on tour.

Momma was always teaching us about our history. She told us of how it was for her in the south. She kept our pride cup filled. She explained how difficult it would be fro us because of the color of our skin. I remembered when Martin Luther King was killed. Momma was crying and explained to us how great a man he was.

She told us of Mary Macleod Bethune, Nat Turner, Jackie Robinson, George Washington Carver, Frederick Douglass, Harriet Tugman, Sojourner Truth, and many other famous and important Blacks. To think of it, that was the only time Momma would look back, in order to resurrect our history for us, for our prides sake.

Momma also made sure we had a foundation in church. She started us in a Baptist church where she was brought up. Momma however was not one of those holier than thou people. After we reached our teens, she allowed us to find our own way within a church. If we went to church that was great, but if we didn't she didn't make a huge fuss about it. Education was her vessel and strong faith was her anchor. Neither one did she force upon us, however both became our foundation.

With a mother such as that I can see why I feel the way I do about my Black women. I admire and respect my mother for what she did for herself. I appreciate even more what she did for me. She gave up much for my sister and me. She was always a tower of strength, aspiration, and love.

I remember Momma telling me I could probably find a good lady in church. Now I wouldn't consider myself a good God fearing devout Christian. At risk of offending some people, I have a hard time justifying a religion that was raped into the lives of my ancestors. Back in Africa, did we believe in Jesus prior to becoming slaves? Were those well to do Christians trying to force God unto savages needing to fear something in order to conform?

My faith is strong and my conviction for doing what is right consistently overtakes me. Momma did the right thing by introducing faith to us young and not forcing it onto us. I firmly believe my faith in God is stronger than if I were forced to believe.

I could quote verse from the Bible, but I don't. I choose not to pass judgment onto my fellow man. At lease, I try not to! I just try to peacefully coexist with my fellow man and keep God a personal yet important private part of my life. Still church was not part of the equation. I could give a myriad of reasons as to why I didn't attend church. The main reason was I felt like a hypocrite.

Half of the people there, I felt, were six-day sinners who hoped by fooling God fifty-two days out of the year they might go to heaven. Sometimes I have to stop and look at myself and wonder who do I think I am. Do I think I'm better than they are? Still that is my reason for avoiding church. Against my better judgment, I decided to take Momma's advice and I went to church to find Ms. Right.

If I felt like a hypocrite before, you can image how I felt now. I was not attending church to find the word. I wasn't there for spiritual healing. I was there for a lady. I became the biggest charlatan there. With all self-loathing aside, I was determined to find the keeper of my hart. That is where I met Marcia.

Marcia sang in the choir. Even more impressive she was the lead vocalist for the church. She had the voice of an angel, and the heart of one. That is how I had the opportunity to meet her. She made it a point to seek out new potential members of the church and make them welcome. I wasn't a regular attendee; I might have gone once or twice a month. After services I did not wait around, I would make a beeline right out of there.

One day out of the blue, as I was making haste to escape the church, Marcia was waiting at the front door and stopped me. She acknowledged seeing me there before and wondered why I didn't come every Sunday. I have to admit I was taken back for a minute. I confess, my intentions in going to church were to find a lady, but I never made an attempt to do so. Out of fear of encounters and escalated hopes, I always left in such a hurry.

At the time, I figured she was trying to commit to more members, doing her job, so to speak. I came up with some lame excuse as to why I did not attend every week and thinking of a way to make my leave as expeditiously as possible, I told her that I would try to make it more frequently.

While talking to Marcia I felt I was moving in two different directions. Part of me was standing there carrying on a conversation I was too nervous to engage. Another part of me was trying to pull away and run like hell. Marcia then innocently reached out and grabbed my arm. At the moment I felt her hand, I felt my two selves zip swiftly together.

My eyes locked onto hers and for a moment in my mind we were the only two people at the church. She looked up at me with her big brown eyes and explained how hard it was to get men to come to church. Marcia went on to tell of how men come only if their wife's force them to come, and even then, they come infrequently.

Marcia expressed her concern for the young black children in the congregation. What message were our men giving? Yes, there were black men there every Sunday; however, the women surely out numbered the men six to one. She pronounced the drama of our youth; particularly our male youth and how lost they are without strong black male role models in church giving support. Marcia revealed how glade she was to see me come alone. She wished more men would do as I.

Boy was she good! Everything she said made good sense to me. By the time we finished talking, not only did I commit honestly to attending more Sundays, I also committed to coming to bible study during the week. The funny thing about my assuring Marcia I would be more committed to the church did not come from a desire for her. I had not given her a second thought. Somehow, I was thinking she was married. I was intensely amazed and affirmed what she was saying. She had struck the right cord in me.

At first, I went to church every Sunday as I promised. I really enjoyed the choir. I would find myself waiting for Marcia to sing her solos. She really had a voice of an angel. Soon after a few weeks, I decided to attend a bible study. I didn't actually know why I decided to go, maybe it was because I wanted to see Marcia, or maybe it was because I had nothing better to do.

I'd never attended a bible study before. I was under the impression that it would be a bunch of people sitting around reading from the bible. To my amazement it was nothing of the sort. Instead of a diatribe of brimstone and walking the straight and narrow, I was overwhelmed with music and people talking about life.

There were a lot of giving thanks, and going to the scriptures for answers, still I felt a little more as ease than I thought I would feel. I was able to interact with the people. Before long, I was feeling part of the flock. It was at bible study Marcia and I began to get closer as friends. At first, we would just talk.

We would talk about our personal dreams and wishes and we would discuss how to help the pastor to grow the church. I offered my services when ever possible. I found myself giving discussions to the children on how to overcome the obstacles of the world. I was beginning to feel my life had a reason and I had Marcia to thank. Had she not grabbed my arm that Sunday and persuaded me to come to church, I wouldn't have felt so good.

Marcia and I grew closer and closer as time lapsed. One day from out of know where Marcia asked me to come over for dinner. My first thought was that she was just offering the invitation out of friendship in the name of good Christian hospitality. My secret desire for her was escalated with great anticipation. I began to hope this was the beginning and the end of my quest to finding my soul mate.

Marcia lived in a modest makeshift garage studio apartment. I somehow felt bad for her for living in such a place. She however seemed very comfortable there. She had fixed it up to have all the comforts of home. We had a nice enjoyable dinner. Marcia was a very good cook. I was beginning to feel things were going in the right direction. I maintained a great deal of constraint; I didn't want to come on too strong. I enjoyed the friendship we had established and did not want to compromise it. Still I wanted in the worst way to just reach out and seize Marcia in my arms and tell her of my hidden feelings for her.

My hopes and dreams were soon destroyed. Right after we ate dinner, Marcia and I sat down to listen to gospel music. She brought out a photo book and started to show me pictures of her and her ex boyfriend J.B. Right then I knew I didn't have a chance. Marcia told me of how they would spend so much time together. She explained how he was a once a key member of the church. She then talked about how he turned away from God and betrayed the church and betrayed her.

J.B. stopped going to church. He started going out with another lady in the church behind Marcia's back. Without any for warning, or common decency J.B. and this other lady were married. Marcia talked of how this tore her apart but that it was God's will. J.B. and this other woman also had a baby, months after their wedding.

I knew right then and there that Marcia was off limits. If she continues to gaze through her photos of J.B. and talks of him with great care, then she is not over him. She explained that J.B. had been married at that time for over a year and still calls once a week. He constantly begs her forgiveness and has regret not only for what he did to her but also regrets getting married.

Then Marcia began to try to convince me that she was over J.B. and as the good, Christian she was could not hold any hatred for him even though he completely destroyed her. Marcia explained that her reason for continuing to talk to J.B. was to help him find Christ again. I am now at the point of wondering why we are having this discussion.

Crushed as I was, realizing I had no chance with Marcia, I offered words of comfort trying to find a tactful way of getting out of there. Just as I fond my way out, Marcia surprised me. She started complimenting me. She said I was a real attractive man and a good Christian man. I was the kind of man she had been looking for. Marcia praised me for not coming on to her as so many other men have. I was now thoroughly shocked.

With the threat of J.B. in the back of my mind, I chose to ignore my feelings of impending doom. Intellectually I knew this could not work with her feelings still strong for J.B. Still I chose to express my true feelings to Marcia. I told her of how I was attracted to her from the start. I expressed how my feelings for her grew every time I hear her sing and how I didn't want to destroy any friendship we had by intruding in a place I didn't feel I was welcome because I wanted to be with her and close to her if only as friends. Marcia then leaned over, kissed me on the cheek, and said that I was truly a good man and she would be honored to be the lady in my life.

I thought this was going to be the start of my happiness instead; this was the start of my heartache. J.B. was the specter that embezzled Marcia's hart. Her father criminally pirated her soul. We had been going out as a couple for a while. We had enjoyed each other's company and I never really made any attempt to be romantic. We'd kissed goodbye and that was the extent of our romance.

One night while cuddled together at my place by the fireplace licensing to music I kissed Marcia on the cheek. I then placed my hand on her other cheek and turned her to me to kiss her on the lips. When I did this, she slightly pulled back. Then she came back and kissed me. Feeling something was wrong, I asked her what it was. Marcia stated nothing was wrong. I apprehensively tried again to kiss Marcia this time on the neck. When I did that she pulled back stronger and told me no!

Frustrated and somewhat angry I asked her if she still had feelings for J.B. As if I had said something so far fetch she replied, what on earth gave you such an insane thought?" I explained to her how I thought that she still was harboring feelings for J.B. because she continues to talk to him after what he did to her.

Marcia stated the only reason she talks to J.B. is to help him find his way back to God. She said there was no way she had feeling of getting back with him. I asked why she kept the photo album out. She stated that she was through with the man but not the memories and I should not expect her to rid her memories just because she is seeing me.

Then Marcia told me a story that turned my stomach. She told me about her father. When she was fourteen her father raped her. Prior to the rape, he would always kiss her on her lips. Even though this made her uncomfortably and asked him not to, he would tell her that is how daddies kiss the ones they loved. Her father was a deacon of their church. He quoted from the bible his justifications. Genesis 48:10 and he kissed them, and embraced them.

I Corinthians 16:20 greet ye one another with a holy kiss.

On her fourteenth birthday, her father came into her room. Marcia's mother was at work at the time. He brought her a birthday present. The present was a set panties with the days of the week inscribed on them. He asked her to try on a pair while he watched. He told her this was the time of her anointing. Fearful Marcia undressed and put on the first pair her hands grabbed.

Her father then asked her to come to him. Wearing nothing but those panties, she approached him. He reached out to her and pulled her to him. He began to kiss her. He started by kissing her on her neck and when he did she began to cry. He said don't cry my love for I'm here to anoint you with the seed of god. You are a young woman and it's my responsibility to instruct you in the ways of the world. He kept kissing her on the neck and about the lips as he quoted what she thought was scripture. Then he started to shiver. While in this state, he stuck his hands into the panties and began to pull them down. He opened his robe to reveal he had nothing on underneath he pulled her on top of him and raped her all the time quoting scripture and kissing her on the neck and about her lips.

For the next three years until he was killed in a car accident, Marcia's father would come into her room every Thursday and anoint her. Marcia never told her mother and to this day, she said, she cannot stand to be kissed in a romantic way. Therefore, J.B. is not anything for me to concern myself about. Marcia stated she enjoyed my company and wanted to be with me, it was just that she could not kiss me in that manner.

After hearing that story, I was terrified of even touching Marcia again. My hart went out to her, yet at the same time I found it very difficult to carry on a normal relationship with her. I like to think of myself as a romantic, I love to cuddle and kiss, sex is wonderful, but I enjoy to foreplay to the exercise of sex. My inability to kiss Marcia made me impotent in romancing her.

I grew increasingly angry with a father who would allow a pair of Thursday's panties and a demented mind destroys his child. I couldn't help but to want her father to be alive so I could torture him for what he did. My mind began to wonder what I got myself into. First I find out Marcia had an ex that betrayed the love, then I find out her father betrayed her innocence. What next?

A few days later Marcia invited me over to her place for dinner. After dinner, we sat down to watch a video. I had my arms around her and was relaxed. Marcia grabbed my hand and placed it on her Brest. At first, I did nothing. I left it there for a while and politely removed it. She again saying nothing placed my hand on her breast again. Marcia had soft voluptuous Brest. This time I started to caress them. I ran my hand ever so slightly over her nipples as they began to harden as show through the shirt.

I began to get aroused as Marcia moaned with pleasure. I leaned over to smell her hair getting even more aroused. Marcia whispered in my ear oh baby you make me feel good! Then she leaned over and kissed me on the cheek. Then she said; make love to me baby.

Completely aroused now, I returned her kiss. I kissed her on the cheek took a whiff of her hair and kissed her on the forehead. Feeling no rejection, I proceeded to caress her face and turned it toward me. I kissed her on the nose and then the lips. Marcia just moaned with pleasure. I kissed her on the cheek again and moved my hand back to her Brest. When I tried to kiss her, again on the lips I got a dead feeling. Marcia looked at me and said AI told you baby I don't like to kiss. My state of arousal immediately left and I went back to watching the video.

Marcia seductively asked me to make love to her again. I told her I couldn't. It will take time for me to be able to get over the fact that I could not kiss her. I informed her that kissing was an important part of love making to me. Marcia then began to plead with me to make love to her. She appeared to be begging so I asked her if all she wanted was sex without it meaning anything to me. She replied that she just wanted to feel me inside of her; she needed me inside of her. I began to feel extremely uncomfortable that I had to say good night and I went home.

Marcia and I saw each other almost every day. Either we met at the church or we met to be together. Every day since that night, Marcia would plead with me to make love to her. Her pleading was excessive and I began to feel bad for not pleasing her.

By now, Marcia and I have known each other for five months. We had been a couple for two months. I liked her a great deal. I felt there were problems with our relationship; J.B. would come up every now and then. The fact that I could not kiss her was a problem but I was determined to find a way over that. Her constant begging me to just screw her made me curious but I knew I wanted it too.

On my birthday, the beginning of our third month as a couple a strange events caused me to really evaluate this relationship. Marcia called inviting me to dinner to celebrate my birthday. When I arrived at her place, she asked if we could go and pick her car up at the repair shop. When we arrived at the repair shop, Marcia asked me to lend her two hundred dollars because she left her money at home.

I have never liked friends to ask for money because that is a sure way to end friendships; however, I lent the money to Marcia. When we got back to her place, she never mentioned the money. She stated where she made reservations and we had to get going. At the restaurant, she asked me to say grace. I am not use to saying grace. Like I said before I keep my faith privet and I would feel awkward saying grace aloud and in public. I told Marcia this and she said; you don't like Jesus!

I was beginning to feel used and abused. First, on my birthday, I give two hundred dollars to have Marcia's car fixed. Then at dinner, my faith is insulted. To add insult to injury when the waitress brought the check, Marcia grabbed it as if to pay it, then she said; that's not too bad, and pushed it back at me. What a birthday!

After dinner back at Marcia's place, she left to bedroom to change. After a few minuets, she called me into the room. When I walked in there, she laid with nothing on at all. Marcia had the body of a Nubian princess. Brown luscious Brest, a narrow waist that led to a pair of delicious full brown legs. She had her right hand down between her legs as if she were preparing herself for me.

I hate to admit it but out of anger more than anything else, I went over to Marcia and started to caress her body. As I moved from her Brest and worked my hands down to the legs and to in-between I became aroused. I then went to kiss her Brest and then she told me no kissing. My anger erupted. My birthday and I have to pay for someone else car to be fixed, I'm insulted regarding my faith, I pay for my birthday dinner, I have not even been told happy birthday, and now I can't make love the way I enjoy to.

At that point, I, in a state of rage ripped my clothes off and gave it to Marcia the way she wanted it. For me it had no meaning, it was not with love, I just slammed into her and like a mad dog I gave it to her repeatedly. Finally, I just turned over and went to sleep.

The next morning I awoke to Marcia kissing and stroking my manhood. When she got it to the point of extreme strength, she mounted me and rode me like a horse. All the time she called the name Jesus. When she was done, she hopped off me, gave me a robe and went to take a shower. I was sitting on the couch when she came out of the shower. Marcia came over to me and said; Baby you really make me feel good." Then she reached down into the robe and began to stroke my manhood again. She began to kiss me on the neck and nibbling my ear.

Once again, she mounted me. I began to feel like an object rather than a person. I was angry that she could kiss me and all I could do was sit there. When she was again done, she instructed me to take my shower while she made breakfast. As I took my shower, I felt extremely dirty. I guessed that most of my friends would love all the sex we were having. I felt dirty; I felt I was betraying myself. I like to make love to a lady not have raw passion if that is what this was.

Marcia was not done. When I came out of the shower, Marcia came into the bathroom and attacked me again. This time she came in to state, she wanted to rub lotion all over my body. I allowed her to and when she got to my loin she stroked in until it grew. She then turned around and leaned over the sink. She started to rub her butt and spread it apart. I cannot deny I got a thrill out of what was happening. I once again serviced her request and we had breakfast.

At breakfast, Marcia asked me if I would like to be a daddy. I suddenly became fearful because we didn't use protection. I wondered why this question was being asked. Marcia stated I was a good man and she would love to have my baby. I told her that I wanted at one time to become a father but only after I find the right lady and get married but now at my age I think I'm too old.

Marcia came back by asking why I did not use a rubber with her if I didn't want children. Feeling trapped and somewhat threaten I lied. I told her I have taken other measures. By now I began to wonder why she had consistently asked, even beg me to sleep whit her. I began to wonder why this lady of God had suddenly become a slut in my eyes. Therefore, I told Marcia I had a vasectomy.

Marcia became flushed when I told her this. She started to cry out, O Jesus, O Jesus! I asked her what was wrong. She cried out AO Jesus no, O Jesus no! I again asked what was wrong. Then Marcia looked at me and told me she was a month pregnant. Stunned, I said what! Marcia told me again she was a month pregnant and the father was J.B.

Marcia went on to state that I was a good responsible Christian man. The kind of man she had been looking for. She thought that if she were to tell me she was pregnant I would take responsibility for the child and marry her. She started back to crying uncontrollably and saying; AO Jesus, O Jesus no!"

I stood up, in rage, I ripped into Marcia; You mean to tell me that last night you told me I didn't love Jesus! All the time you were planning to commit such a deceit! You call yourself a born again Christian! You have the gull to question my faith! You were sleeping with a married man while dating me! Then you were ready to ruin my life with such deceit! You thought I was that dumb not to be able to count the months! You make me sick to my stomach!" I got up and walked out to never return.

As I walked to my car, I could still hear her crying and begging for forgiveness. I felt like a heal. I felt dirty. I felt like God was punishing me for going to church for the wrong reasons. I finally said to myself what I had not been told in the last twenty-four hours. Happy birthday!

REFLECTIONS
WHY AM I ALONE?

I sit at home all alone watching my cat. Loneliness has not been pleasant. I got a cat because he keeps me company when all else seems bleak. I can't have a loveable dog where I live. The space I have cannot accommodate such a pet. A cat is not a bad companion he has an independence I envy. Even though he needs me, he can find pleasure in being alone, and for that matter, he is good at showing me that fact at times.

My cat represents another fact. He represents the only pussy I will see for a long time. Not that I'm looking for a lady to only fulfill my sexual needs. I could satisfy those needs with any tramp in the street. Sex still is an important part of a relationship and anyone denying that is lying.

As I sit home alone, I ask myself, what is wrong with me? Why am I living a life of loneness? When I look in the mirror, I see an attractive man. I'm not Denzel Washington, yet I look pretty damn good. I take my clothes off and I see a body that any man would be proud of. I work out often and spent plenty time taking care of myself, yet I'm still alone.

I have a flourishing career. I have climbed the latter of success and I'm proud of my accomplishments, yet I'm still all alone. It is baffling. You would think I am what a Black lady wants. I thought so, but here I sit, two bachelors, my cat and I watching the walls, not having any contact with a love.

It is a mistake to believe that all brothers are out there with many women on the side. It is said there are five Black women to every one Black man. If you take in account all the brothers in jail, or who are gay, you would think I would have no problem finding just one lady for myself. Some of the brothers out there must have much more than their share, for I am without one.

I have a very close friend that means a lot to me. She is a beautiful person. When we get together, we can talk about anything. Often we flirt with each other, playing dangerous games that could damage our friendship. To be honest she likes me, and would drop her pants if I would make a genuine move at her. If I am so lonely, why don't I take her into my life?

Well, she is a good friend and I do not want to loose that bond. That is what I keep telling myself. If I believe that then I believe my own bullshit. The truth is she happens to be a little overweight. Aha, the truth comes out! Does that make me superficial? Am I no better than the other dogs out there?

If she is such a good person, and she is. If she makes me happy, and she does. Why must her weight push me away? I guess I am a bit superficial. All of us are. If I looked like a genetic experiment, would she want me? Is this not truth or is it more self-preservation bullshit? Maybe that is why I'm alone.

I am told I should be able to find a lady at work. What I run into are those fly girls! Women with fake hair, fake nails, wearing tons of war paint. These women walk around with a train of papooses trailing behind them. The papooses who are the children of low life homeies that have fucked the ladies in more ways than one. Do I think I am any better? I guess I'm a snob, Maybe that is why I'm alone.

Other women I run into at work are snobs, like me. I'm not a Doctor or a Lawyer. I don't drive a BMW or a Mercedes. My hair is not styled in a fashion they like. My cloths do not come from the covers of GQ. I am not their idea man. Turnabout is fair play I guess. If I judge women as a snob, then it is only fair I secure judgment in the same manner. Maybe that's why I'm alone.

Do I need a lady to justify my life? I am so lonely and needy that sometimes I feel sick. My search for a good Black lady becomes more and more obsessive as each day passes. Friends and family tell me often to stop looking. "When you stop looking the lady of your dreams will come along." I just can't stop looking since my pain is so deep. Maybe my desperation explains why I'm alone.

My desperation stimulates foolhardy expeditions. I venture out to clubs. I know this is a feudal quest but I do it anyway. There I find people acting in the play of life. Single life has spawned many people like me who are lonely yet fearful of closeness. We fear that person who seems nice and talks good yet has other motives.

At clubs, I find sisters who have been dogged by my brothers. They tend to be afraid of me, yet they too are lonely. What ends up happening is we put on an act of sparing. Ladies gather at clubs in packs of male bashing hateful creatures. Men gather as a swarm of lust filled egocentric grafters. Both parts are played out in a game of deprivation.

I sit back and watch the primitive mating rituals. I watch the home boys glide up to women. He sticks out his hand as if the national signal for let's dance is a hand stuck out low, and the head tilted just slightly to the right. Without saying a word, he expects the lady to dance with him. If she does, he then looks at this as a sign of her saying yes you can fuck me tonight.

If she does not respond, he must go into faze two and come up with a line that will cause her to wet her panties. "Yo baby you sho look like you know how to make a man hurt." This really means: "I have very little respect for myself, and even less respect for you, so let's go somewhere and fuck!"

Brothers are not the only players in this game of nighttime roulette. Sisters have their role to play as well. When a women dance with a man she is telling him that she is lonely and needs a man even if for just a moment. She is also saying: "Yea baby I'm shaking my good stuff all in your face so you will know just what you won't be screwing!"

When she tells a brother she is too tired to dance, she is really telling the brother: "Baby, You are a tired fool! I wouldn't dance with your cornbread fed ass if you were the only man on earth." As I look at the melodrama unfold I cannot help but to laugh. At the same time, I cry, for this does not help me fulfill my need. I closed the curtain on the club scene. I'm not looking to be an actor in this tragedy. Maybe that is why I'm alone.

I take another bold step. I try groceries stores, laundry mats, and other such avenues that I hear are good places to meet women. I find this is not the answer because most women feel invaded when they are approached openly like that. I must be thought of as one of those scamming brothers who have no respect for their privacy. These places are better than clubs are if you want to get laid, but they are not a place to find a good lady. The good ones just want to be left alone.

By now, you must be thinking I am one ugly brother with many hang-ups. Not quite. I am attractive and I am a proud Black man who has much to offer a lady. I hear all the time how hard it is to firm a decent Black man these days. I feel I fit the prescription very well. Still I find myself alone.

When I am lucky enough to find a special strong Black lady, I have other problems. Because you are constantly saturated with men who are nothing better than scoundrel is, you are not accustom to the handling you deserve. I suffer because you question my sexual preference when I don't try to rip your cloths off. I can't count the many times I have been called a faggot because I don't treat you like a whore.

I try to be a gentleman. You claim you would appreciate a man who will treat you right. You claim you want someone who is honest and caring. That is exactly who I am. My reward, you call me a faggot. Worse yet you tell me that I am too good for you. I have suffered my greatest heartache from women who have told me I was too good for them. Have you been laying with dogs so much that you have forgotten your own value? I sometimes wish I too were a scoundrel for then I will not be alone. I'm not a dog however. Maybe that's why I'm alone.

I find myself taken for a fool by women who think my kindness is a weakness. If I am not thought of as a dog then I find myself being treated as one. Well I may be a nice guy, but I am not a fool. I don't need a lady that bad as to allow one to take advantage of me. Maybe that's why I'm alone.

I have tried personal ads. 'Single Black Man, articulate, educated, and professional. Seeks SBF who is contemporary traditional, must be independent and strong, for a lasting relationship.' Now I think to myself, this will be the answer. After all, retailers advertise to get what they want. Maybe now I will find Ms. Right.

The personals only engendered beautiful, dysfunctional, insecure, and fearful women who have had too many tormented relationships with my fellow brothers. I lived through painful stories of how my counterparts treated them with little esteem. I endured story after story of male debasement. I even suffered from a fatal attraction. I realized that personal ad's is the last frontier for the desperate. I found that desperation caused many very fine ladies to loose self-respect. This was the perception I got from personals. I may be lonely, but I'm not that desperate yet.

Here I sit all alone without a beautiful Black lady to comfort me. I called myself trying to find the answers. I journeyed all the venues I knew trying to find you. Still I come home to an empty home.

I asked my sister, "Yo what's up with me. What is it I'm doing wrong?" She tells me of how there are no 'good men' out there, and Black women are feed up with trying to give us a chance. She tells of how she and her girlfriends get together and cry in their beer.

If it is true there aren't any good men out there, then I should be a welcome treasure. When I look at my brothers with White women, when I see the home-boy types with women dripping off them, I cannot help but to be envious. Still I will not change, for I think there is a Beautiful Black lady out there for me. As you, My Sisters continue with your struggle in the daily battle of existence, remember, Brother To Sisters, there are a few of us Black men who are not of the barbarian type.

There are a few good Black men who welcome the strength and beauty you represent. There are those of us who will not settle for anything other than having a Black lady in our lives. You have suffered much and may suffer much more. If you continue to be strong, one day your man may wake up and help launch you to the level of queen as you are destine to be.

CHAPTER TWO
STRIKE ONE

Desperate feelings lead to desperate actions. Brenda was a beauty I found a work. Static's show that fifty percent of matches are made at the work place. That obviously didn't work for me. I compromised my professional ethics to make a go with Brenda and that didn't work. She made it impossible for me to consider that again. Most criminals are caught because they are dumb enough to keep trying to commit the same crime. Sexual harassment didn't look like an option for me.

Church was a bad idea. I went there to find that church people with all their great love of God and scriptures play the same polluted games as those in the world. Marcia's quick judgment of those who did not believe as her was in my opinion contradictory to the teachings of the bible. Her adultery and willingness to deceive was an evil that was unforgivable to me.

What was I suppose to do? Where was I going to find my Ms. Right? You hear about meeting people at the grocery store. When I go shopping, I go to do just that and nothing else. I guess I am supposed to run my shopping cart into some lovely ladies cart and stay; Excuse me. Nice to see you eat wheat bread, can I have your number?" That just does not work for me. When at the store I just want to get in and out. I find it hard to believe that anyone else would have anything other on their minds but the same.

Laundry mats I have no use for. I have a washing machine and dryer at home. Bars and nightclubs turn me off because I don't like drunks. I am not willing to play the dating game. There is a completely different language spoken at these places. I am not able to properly interpret the correct hand signals, eye gestures, and body maneuvers.

A friend told me to try personal ads. She told me that she went to a class about how to meet men and the instructor mentioned this was a very good way to sift though all the bad seeds in the single market. She also told me she had done it and was successful. She met a nice guy who was in the service. They had been going out for a month and everything was going fine.

My first thought about personal ads was that they were full of people who were sexually perverse. If that weren't their claim to fame, they were social rejects who were unable to communicate with the world face to face; pathetic dysfunctional wrecks whose lives were so bad that they had to resort to selling themselves in a newspaper.

My friend explained to me that the people in the personals were like us. People who work too much, who are tired of bars, and do not want to be seen as meat in the market. People who are willing to take time and invest in really weeding out the garbage. Personals offer you that opportunity. You state what you are looking for and when you get responses, you can talk to the people in the comfort of your home. You then have the ability to make a qualified chose without any hassles. By the time you meet, you have already made some kind of connection.

Feeling somewhat convinced I placed a personal ad, after all what could it hurt:

Pride Soaring;

SBM 33 seeks prideful traditionally strong SBF, not looking for conquest or conflict; let's let our flowers grow in the same garden, no games and please no children.

I felt very proud of myself. I thought I had written a very good ad for myself. It stated just enough about me and what I was looking for. I still did not feel too optimistic about what was going to respond but I was looking forward to the experience.

The ad ran for two weeks every Tuesday in a local throw away newspaper. I received five responses to the ad. The first troublesome thing I found was how easy it was to discount another human being. The first lady was Rose. Rose sounded like she hated men or at best had a difficult time with my fellow Black brothers. Her response to my ad was; hi, my name is Rose, I am a thirty three year old SBF, like you, I'm tired of the lies people tell you. I'm sick of the games. If you are looking to jump my bones, you are barking up the wrong tree!" Rose was out.

The second was Marry, she responded; Hello I'm Marry, I'm a forty two year old SBF, I have no kids at home and I would love to plant myself next to you in you garden."

I guess my ad wasn't that good after all. I did not put in an age range nor did I state that I was looking for a lady who hadn't any children. I was not prepared to date someone older than me. Since I did not have children, I wanted someone who made the same choices as I. Marry was out.

As I stated, it became disturbingly easy to discount people. I continued down the list. The next was Valerie. Valerie's response was not bad however, she sounded like a ghetto girl. This is what I mean about how disturbing it was to discount someone without knowing them. Just on her voice alone and how she pronounces her words, I discounted Valerie.

Left now with only two choices I became desperate. This couldn't fail. I had no faith in personal ads yet I became obsessed with trying to find at lease one connection. The next was Velma. The name alone did not sound right to me yet I wasn't going to ax her out just because of the name. Her response to my ad appeared to be genuine. Her voice was sexy and she articulated properly. She was a year older that I, never married and had no children.

The last choice was Sheila. Sheila was the same age as I and never married, no children and sounded very sweet. Her response to my ad was the most sincere of all. Out of the five Sheila was the one I thought would be pay dirt. Sheila was the first I called.

I had already made a list of things I would not want to hear in conversation. I didn't want hear the question, what kind of car I drove? I didn't want the conversation to go to sex. I did not want references to money. These things I thought were the fishing questions women asked if they were gold digging. Sheila and I talked the first time for five hours. I have never stayed on the phone that long before. We had an enjoyable conversation. We talked about everything imaginable.

After talking to Sheila, I was so excited. Maybe there was some value to personal ads. I couldn't wait to talk to her again. Since Sheila and I hadn't made a date, I thought I might give Velma a call the next day.

Velma and I hit it off right away as well. We only talked on the phone for two hours when Velma asked if we could meet. We agreed to get together and go to the beach. With one date secured, I thought I would call Sheila and see if I could make a date with her. When I got on the phone with her, it was as if we had known each other forever. The conversation flowed with ease. I wanted to meet her in the worse way. The problem was she was always too busy. We could talk on the phone for hours yet could not find time to get together.

The time came for Velma and me to get together. I went over to her place to pick her up. I ashamed to say she did match her name. Velma was five foot four inches tall. Her breast was the size of watermelons and had a butt to match. She had to be pushing 170lbs. most of which was in her Breast a butt. It was too late for me to back out of the date and I was mortified with myself for being so shallow.

In the car on our way to the beach, Velma asked me a question I could not believe at first. Tell me, she said, what turns you on?

Excuse me! I replied.

I just want to know what turns you on sexually. You are a very attractive man and I want to make sure I please you.

I am thinking to myself, we've only talked on the phone for two hours. Seen each other for only fifteen minuets, and now she wants to turn me on sexually. What have I gotten myself into now? I didn't answer her question. I told her we need to get to know one another better first. The rest of the way to the beach we talked about other subjects but I was thinking of how to end this date fast. I was thinking of Sheila knowing we would not be in this kind of predicament.

I happen to enjoy the beach at night. I figured I would not have any trouble sitting and watching the stars and listening to her waves. I laid out a blanket and brought out a radio. We sat talking for a while. My friends tell me that my honesty is like a chain saw cutting into flesh. I could not tell this lady she turned me off the minuet I saw her, and her first comment was a further turn off.

Before I knew it, Velma leaped at me and jammed her tongue down my throat. She grabbed at my groin and began to squeeze and shake at my loin. I had to push her off. She requested to turn me on and again attacked me. Her squeezing and yanking was painful and her kisses smelt of spoiled milk. After pushing her off again, she asked if I wanted a blowjob! I told her outside at the beach was not a good place for that kind of thing. She then requested to go to my place where she could make me feel really good. I told her I had better take her home and we could start over another day. I took her home, and with apprehension, I kissed her good night. Velma was out.

I immediately ran home a called Sheila on the phone. We talked again for hours but I could not get her to commit to a date. After two weeks of talking on the phone, I finally got Sheila to commit to a date. The night of our date, I called Sheila up to find out how I would know her since we were going to meet at a neutral location.

Up until now, we had never talked about how we looked. She asked me to describe myself. I told her I was six feet three inches tall and about 215lbs. with an athletic build since I work out everyday. She told me she was five foot eight inches tall but not athletic. Then she got very quiet. Sheila's quiet was very noticeable that I asked her what was wrong.

She said there was nothing wrong then asked how I like my women.

I told her I liked them nice, like her. She responded by repeating she wasn't athletic. Feeling she was about to cancel the date because she thought I would not like her, I told her I like all kinds of women. I told her I was not looking for a skinny rail nor was I looking for a Ms. Olympia. I wanted to impress upon her that she was what I was looking for. Sheila still was quiet. Finally, I asked if she did not want to meet. She paused for a moment and said; I guess we can meet.

When I arrived at the restaurant, I decided to wait outside. I figured, why go inside and risk the embarrassments of being stood up. I chose a restaurant that few Blacks went to so I would know Sheila when she came up. Twenty minuets after our scheduled time I was ready to leave thinking Sheila was not going to show, when a very attractive lady pulled into the parking lot.

When she got out of the car, I got out of mine and we knew right away, whom we were. She was right she was not athletic but she carried herself well. I was pleased with what I saw. I told her I was glad she came, and that I was pleased with what I saw. She told me she started not to come but after seeing me, she was glad she came.

Inside the restaurant I ordered an appetizer and ice tea. Sheila said she wasn't hungry and ordered a Margarita. All the time we sat at the table Sheila would pull at her cloths as if to cover up. I could tell she was as nervous as a prostitute in church. Her lower lip kept shivering. She kept looking at the appetizers but would not take one. I tried everything in my power to make her feel at ease. I complimented her, I tried to be funny but every thing I did failed.

I reached over to grab her hand once while we were talking and when I looked into her eyes, it was like a deer standing in front of headlights. I could not help but to feel that somehow I did this to Sheila. She would talk, but all the time grabbing at herself. I really liked her and thought she was attractive. I kept getting the feeling she did not think herself good enough.

The next day I called Sheila and got her answering machine. I left her a message but it was never returned. I tried calling her a few more times only to get the same response. Sheila was out.

Out of desperation, more than anything I went back to my list of rejected calls. I decided to give Valerie a chance. The gull of me to think I was doing her a favor by *giving her a chance.* The so call ghetto girl was my only hope to make this personal ad experience a success. When I herd her phone ring, I felt contempt for myself. Here I had already discounted her because of my bias thoughts and now I'm counting on her to fulfill my lonely void.

While talking to Valerie it became obvious that my first impression of her was wrong. She sounded like a nice lady. I have to admit I was a bit apprehensive at first. I hated myself for prejudging her, and I resented talking to her because I felt my first impression was right. I was fooling myself by talking to her. Valerie soon eased my contempt. She was two years older than I was. She was a full time student and working part time.

Valerie had been married before but had no children. She was like a refreshing dose of reality. I was thinking we were from two different worlds. God only knows why I would think such a thing. I grew up in the hood. I was able to make a successful run at life while my homies were unable to. Most of the men I ran with in the neighborhood were killed, in jail, or on crack. That however makes me no better than they because I was able to overcome the hurdles.

Talking to Valerie on the phone I soon realized she was probably just what I needed. She had no pretense about herself. She didn't carry airs nor did she make excuses. This ignorant ghetto girl, I so arrogantly prejudged, and I talked from 9:00pm until 5:00am. Once we got on a roll, we could not stop. We talked about any and everything. I guess you can say we hit it off pretty good. We had such a good time talking to each other that we agreed to meet that same day for dinner.

When I finally met Valerie, I was knocked over. She looked just like Anita Baker. She had the cutest little full lips. Her eyes were like bashful pools of sweet chocolate, and her smile would put the sun to shame. I was very pleased. We sat to have dinner and that went just as good as I could have ever hoped.

I asked Valerie about her marriage. I did not want some ex of hers coming around to settle things with me. Valerie told me a story of a Black man who after loosing his job went down hill. He started using drugs. He spent more time in the streets than at home with his wife. Never trying to find another job, he just blamed the white man for his ills and hung out with riff raft. It didn't take long for him to start blaming Valerie for his problems. He started beating on her.

With all of that, Valerie continued to stay with him. She thought he might get himself back together. As time went on the beatings got worse. When he found out she was pregnant he beat her into a miscarriage. Still she stayed. She said she had been with this man for ten years. They had a house and a lot of good furniture she took a long time getting right. He didn't want her to work and she enjoyed being a housewife. It was hard for her to give all that up. She thought it would be just as hard for him as well so she stuck around for him to come back.

It all came to a head when one day he came home and picked a fight with her for no reason. He began to beat on her, kick her, and throw her around. Finally, he picked her up by the neck and chocked her until she went out. When she woke, he was not there. She got up, left, and never returned. She did not take cloths, money, anything; she left everything behind and moved to California where she had relatives. She got a divorce and has been starting over since then.

Valerie's mother still condemns her to this day for leaving a house full of furniture. Her mother felt Valerie should have stuck it out with the man. That is why she left the state and moved to where her aunt lived. When she first told her mother where she was, her mother sent the husband after her. Valerie told me that she and her mother still don't have a good relationship. Her mom is still mad at her for getting a divorce.

After dinner, we went to the pier to walk around. I liked Valerie so much I did not want the date to end. We walked along the beach, stopped to cuddle on the rocks to hear the wave's crash. We held hands, we hugged and we did a lot of kissing. Regretfully the night drew to an end. I drove Valerie home. I was ready to kiss her goodnight at the door when she invited me in. We felt right together and neither of us wanted to end the night. I finally told her I had better go so we will not ruin such a good date by moving too fast.

From that night on, we were together every day. We used every reason to be together. Valerie had no car, so every time she had an errand to run I offered to take her. We did her laundry together, her shopping, and whatever she had to do. I would pick her up from school and bring her home. One night after I brought her home she offered to make me dinner. I knew she was tired so I offered instead to make cheese popcorn and we could watch a video.

That night when she offered me to stay I did. That night was the most wonderful night I spent. We just held each other. I love to tell stories so I told stories and we laughed. We kissed, we laughed we kiss some more. Nothing else happen. I just told her stories until she fell asleep. That night I watch Valerie, my Nubian queen as she slept in my arms until finally I fell asleep.

The next morning we awoke and smiled at each other. I had not felt this way in a long time. As she crawled over me to get to the bathroom so she could take her shower, I grabbed her and pulled her back into bed. For the next hour, we made such passionate love that we were both late for work and did not care. That whole day I had such a smile on my face that everyone noticed. Valerie said she was going through the same feeling.

I felt I had hit the jackpot. Just to think I would have lost this happiness had I followed through on my first impression of Valerie's response to my ad. I love old black and white movies of romance. When guy meets girl and brakes out into song, when one foot was on the floor. Long have I waited for finding that special lady that could make a smile cross my face though I am miles from her. Valerie was that lady.

Valerie and I were from different worlds. She had spent most of the adult life in a marriage that was based on her dependence of a man. She had not traveled much as I had. She had never had a job until she left the marriage. She led a simple existence of going to movies as her only entertainment. I exposed her to new experiences.

I remember I told her I was going to take her to a very special dinner. I told her she had to dress up and not question me about the dinner. I planed to take her to a mystery dinner. There we would have dinner and suddenly find ourselves entangled in a murder we were to solve. I figured Valerie would get a kick out of this but I kept it a secret.

When I got over to Valerie's apartment that night, it was as if she was a high school senior on her way to the prom. She had her girlfriend over to help her dress. Valerie looked so beautiful when she dressed up. In any case, Valerie and her girlfriend were giggling and running around that I got a kick watching them.

After we arrived at the hotel where the dinner was being held, I told Valerie what she was in for. I told her that at the party mixer before we sat to dinner she had to mingle with the other guess in order to try to see who the murderer is. If she felt like it, she could lie to the other guess to make them think she might be the one. Valerie jumped into character as if she was a seasoned actress.

I enjoyed showing Valerie the things she had not experienced before. We went to plays. We went on harbor cruises. We went hiking in the mountains of San Gabriel. We did much more than sit around as couch potatoes and go to an occasional movie. We also could not keep our hands off each other. Making love to Valerie was an experience I have not been able to recapture again.

That brings me sadly to the end of this wonderful chapter of my life. For three wonderful months, Valerie and I were inseparable. I would spend my nights at her place or she would spend her nights at my place. I was looking forward to us being together forever. Then we had our first disagreement. Until now, we never once fought over anything. We were like soul mates that belong together.

One day Valerie brought up the subject of children. She wanted to have some. She gave the biological clock reasoning. She thought we might think of having children. I love children. In my youth, I wanted to have two, a boy and a girl. I wanted a girl most of all. I knew that if I had a girl I would spoil her much. She would be the rain that nourish my fields, and I would chariest her for that reason. I wanted a boy purely out of ego.

This I told to Valerie, however I added the truth of biology. We were of an age that would not be good for a child. I asked her how she would feel to have a thirteen year old at fifty. The truth of the matter was that I have acquired a certain amount of independence. I knew that I would give that up if I had to raise a child for the next eighteen plus years. I wanted to retire young and travel more.

I wanted to write. I wanted to share my love with no other than lady of my life. I had planed to take a month or two to travel the full continent of our motherland Africa. This I could not do if I had a child to care for, set, and mold the life of for eighteen years. I did not explain this to Valerie but I did not have to. She knew what I was feeling before I thought it.

I did however tell her that we were too old to consider children. I told her of my dysfunctional family. How I did not want to reproduce such genes. From laziness to greed, from disassociation to envy, from persecution to the killing of babies, I would pass down to a child this legacy. I told her I wanted children when I was young but now I did not know.

Valerie told me she never considered she was too old to have children. She became extremely distant from that point. As she could feel my deep thoughts, I could just as well feel hers. I realized what I just said destroyed her hopes. I did not know how to take back what I felt and said. I tried unsuccessfully to convince her that I would be glade to have children with her when the time was right. I told her when she finished school and get her degree we could consider it.

I knew this didn't make things better. Valerie was thinking along the lines of becoming a housewife. She saw me as the provider while she took care of the home. That night Valerie stayed at my home. That was the first night she didn't sleep in my arms. The next day I took her to work. I didn't hear from her that day and I could not reach her for three days.

When I finally reached her, she told me that she had to do some thinking. She told me that everything was fine. This was not true however; we no longer saw each other every day. It was almost as if I had to make an appointment to see her. She stayed distant when we were together. I felt I lost her and did not know how to get her back.

One Saturday night Valerie called. She was drunk and I could hear music and a lady in the background. She told me she had her cousin over and they had a little to drink. Not being a drinker myself and not liking people who are drunk I told her to give me a call tomorrow. Out of the background screamed the voice of Valerie's cousin. Is that the rich bastard with the Mercedes and the house? Tell him to come over I'll fuck him if you wont!

Valerie told her cousin to keep quiet but it was too late. I herd what her cousin said. I asked Valerie what she meant by what she said. Valerie tried to pass it off, as her cousin was drunk and did not know what she was talking about. I told Valerie good-by and hung up the phone.

Everybody that knows me knows I never say good-by. When I said it to Valerie, I didn't mean it at the time. Subconsciously I did mean it. We had become very distant. Here it was Saturday night and I was alone while she drank and got drunk at home. It was bad enough that she distanced herself from me, but now I find out that she had lowered me to just a man of means rather than a man of love for her. Rich bastard, house, Mercedes, is that all I was to her? Her cousin would not have said those things without Valerie saying them first.

The next day Valerie left a message on my phone. I was there I just didn't answer. She asked if I said good-by to her last night or was she mistaken. I never returned her call. I guess that was bad of me. I could not get over the cements of her cousin. I could never feel again that Valerie liked me or liked what I might have represented. Valerie was out

CHAPTER THREE
NO CHILDREN

I want you to meet a friend of mine. He just went through a divorce. His wife and kids live in Chicago and he just moved here, he is looking for someone to keep company with.

A friend of mine gave this line to a lady friend of his. He had good intentions of setting me up with someone he thought I would like. Of course, everything he told her was a complete boldface lie. The only thing he got right was that I was from Chicago. Although I had been in California then for over nine years, I asked him why he told such a gigantic lie. His answer was just as disturbing and pathetic as my needing him to set me up.

"Well, ya no. I didn't want her to think there was something wrong with you. Ya no what I'm saying. I didn't want her to think you were some kind of faggot or looser. A man at your age with no kids, gots ta have something wrong with em. You see. I know you and know what kind of man you are. She is a good lady and I wanted you two to get together. What was I supposed to tell her? She asked me if you had any kids. I didn't want you to look bad." Was his response to me.

I was amazed by his logic. "Now James," I went on to say, "you mean to tell me that if you told this lady I was a decent professional man. I had a good moral foundation. I had no children because I have never been married. I am looking to get married some day when I find the right lady. To the best of your knowledge I have never treated a lady wrong, never hit a lady, never cursed out a lady, all of these truths would not make her interested?"

"Hell no! Man that shit don't work!" James responded. "You want the bitch to go out with you. Don't you? If I told her all that bullshit, she would think I'm either lying or she would really think there was something wrong with you." James continued.

Needless to say, I never went out with James's friend. I did get the chance one day to meet her. James brought her by my job. He asked me to come out to his car because he had someone for me to meet. When I went out to the car, there sat a woman in a very short dress that I could see all her glory as she got out to meet me. On the seat between them was a bottle of Jack that was half-gone.

I was pleasant. I said hi to her while behind her back James was winking at me. We talked a wile and I told her I would get her number from James and that maybe we would get together. Without much delay, I went back to work. I could not help to think that she was in a married mans car early in the morning with an open bottle of whiskey. No wonder she would not believe the truth about me. James told me she had two children. Knowing James as I do, I would not be surprised if one of them were his.

"Everybody is entitled to one mistake." Some would say.

I guess it is a mistake to open your legs and expose your ancestry to any seed carrier that comes along with the right words but the wrong actions. It is surely a mistake to have a baby to entrap, keep, or bond a man to in your life that has laid seed with other women. You thought you would be different. Truly, it is a mistake to live with or marry someone, expose your ancestry, then find out years later he is a vagrant. *No es mi problama*

"I was too young when I had my baby. I didn't know any better."

Funny how the early dawns ignorance, makes the rest of the day interminable. Young wilds that lead to a pregnancy could be attributed to ignorance. One can say it was that one mistake you are entitled to. It is criminal how my generation has set the precedence of teenage pregnancy. Those of us who are in their thirties in the nineties with teenagers that are having babies have set this genocide in motion. Blame it on ignorance if you wish. Funny isn't it how I was able to know better? There are many more like me who knew better.

I am constantly held in contempt because I say I don't want to date a woman with children. To err is human, to forgive divine. To take responsibility for someone else error is dire. Many women with children say they are not looking for a person to take care of their child. That can't be further from the truth. In order to be with that lady you have to take on the responsibility of that child as well.

You have to include the child in your plans or risk being responsible for the child's neglect. You end up feeding, providing entertainment and buying gifts for the child. To prove her independence the mother often forbids your interference in the decision making.

"That's my baby not yours! He **HAASS** a father! Don't talk to my child like that!" these are statements from women with children to you.

If there is a father in the child's life, he becomes a more active player once you come on the scene. A man refuses to allow another man in his child's life. You now are forced to carry the baggage of that other man who slept with your lady. You become familiar with the phrase!

"My baby's father this, or my baby's father that." The ghost of the baby's father always looms near. He comes up in conversation more times than you want.

If there is not a father in the child's life, the specter looms ten fold. The child becomes so attached to its mother that it will do anything to sabotage the relationship. The odds are that the child has seen many men come into the mother's life only to hurt her in the end. Maybe the child became attached to a man in its mother's life.

The man left without any notice because he did not get along with the mother. The child is often left unaware as to why he is gone and it is hurt by the experience. Now, you come along and to prevent from getting hurt again the child rebels.

The phrase, "you aren't my daddy!" is a difficult expression to overcome. The phrase, "you aren't my daddy!" is a difficult expression to overcome. I am not my brother's seed keeper.

"Fool me once shame on you. Fool me twice shame on me." One day I will always hate is "**MOTHERS DAY**." That is the day when government checks arrive. That is also the day when black men prostitute their loins for money. I see many of my beautiful Black ladies running to cash their checks. Trailing along behind them are the children they conceived by some dead beat. I would also see those dead beats coming out of the wood works looking to get money.

Many of my lovely Black sisters spent most of the month without a man to partner with. They are forced to care for their children alone. They spend a lot of time with girlfriends talking about how bad men are. Yet on **"mother's day"** and for a few days after they subject themselves again into spreading their ancestry to a man that cares only for his five minutes of pleasure. The results often are another life is condemned to be brought forth.

I don't like making these statements. I feel bad for passing judgment on my Black queens. I'm not God to past judgment but I am the one that has to live my life. I have not foolishly spread my seed. I have not taken a wife to discount her after vowing before God, until death do us part. I have never caused an abortion. I have never struck a lady. I have never betrayed the trust of a lady. These are qualities I would hope my Black queens would desire.

Just because I seek these same qualities in the lady I wish to spend forever with, I'm treated as an outcast. I'm not dumb enough to think I will find an angelic virgin to wed. Is it too much to ask for a lady who made thoughtful choices? A lady who choices were to wait for the right man? A lady who decided not to allow just any man access to the eggs of her ancestry? Is it too much to ask a queen to say…

"I will not wed until I know my king will do right by me?"

I know it is not a prefect world. I know we cannot always make the right choices. Some mistakes can be avoided. Some errors are inexcusable. All that is required of you is to kiss the frog to see if he transform into a prince. You do not have to lie down with him. The tongue wagging of the frog only speaks to catching flies. Wait for your prince to speak before you dub him king. Like the Black Widow my queens should say; "Honor me not, and I will devour you!"

The great scholar Shaftsbury once wrote:

"The greatest of fools is he who imposes on himself, and in his greatest concern thinks certainly he knows that which he has least studied, and of which he is most profoundly ignorant."

I do not profess to know the answer. I realize judgment comes from God not from me. My Black queens need not apologize to me for their errors, mistakes, or choices. I also need not to make apology for what my choices have been or will be. I have not made my choice out of judgment but from experience.

My first experience with a lady with a child was back in Chicago. Her name was Melba. Melba was a nursing student. We met a dinner party that was given by a singles club. Even back then, I was a workaholic. I was a full time student also working full time.

The one thing I missed most about Chicago for the time I spent in California was the community. This singles club I belonged to was sponsored by one of the local nightclubs. This nightclub was one of many clubs in Chicago that Black professionals could go and unwind with their own community. I don't recall ever seeing anything other than Blacks in this club.

California on the other hand is the Mecca of interracial mating. I saw many a proud Black Brothers arrive in California, never once thinking of dating white, suddenly dating everything but a sister. It was impossible to find a professional nightclub that catered exclusively to Blacks. That is why I eventually left La La Land in order to go south where my roots were.

Getting back to Melba, she and I met one night at the club and like all first contacts; we talked, got to know one another and finally exchanged phone numbers. Melba had one of the sexiest voices I have ever heard. We went out a couple of times and I never once knew she had a daughter.

It did not matter in those days to me weather or not she had any kids. I was just a wild buck with the whole world in the palms of my hand. I was looking for action rather than a life long partner. One street in Chicago had a strip of motels that charged by the hour. This was because most of us wild bucks would frequent these places for a little tail and go off to the races. These rooms might be cleaned and turned over to the next buck to arrive.

Living at home with mom was why I knew these places well. The first thing I liked about Melba was she lived on her own. I knew I would be saving a little extra money by not having to go to the motel. After what I said earlier, this must sound awfully bad.

"Well I was a young toad. I didn't know any better." Ha!

On about our third date Melba asked me over. She wanted to make me dinner. I thought, "This was good," I was about to get laid. I made myself up and went over to Melba's without haste. That was when I learned to my surprise Melba had a daughter.

When the door opened there stood a cute little girl of about ten years old.

"Christopher is here," she yelled out as she let me in and closed the door. The little girl then ran off to a room in the back.

"I didn't know you had a daughter!" I exclaimed to Melba when she came to great me.

"Yes. That's my little pride and joy. I wouldn't know what I would do with myself if I didn't have her." Melba responded

"Well Melba needless to say I'm a little surprised." I said in turn.

"There's nothing to be surprise about. You have nothing to do with her."

With that last comment the little girl, whose name I never knew, came running out of her room with a backpack and some clothes.

"I guess that means I'm spending the night downstairs huh mom." Without ever saying a word to me, off she went.

That night at dinner Melba and I enjoyed the entertaining antics of her gay neighbors over dinner. They would scream at one another. They would curse one another. They had sex with each other. All of which you could hear from Melba's apartment.

After dinner, we sat on the couch and in a matter of seconds; we were going at it as if this was going to be our last. Repeatedly we went at it. In the living room, we got sweaty to the bedroom, and even in the bathroom. Finally just as the sun was about to come, we stopped.

The next day I called Melba but we never talked again after that. I could not ever get off my mind what that little girl said. Later it would haunt me, what kind of life this little girl was exposed to. What kind of respect would this girl have for a mother, that whenever a man would come over, she knew she had to leave because mom would be on her back all night. How many men had she met before? How long did it take her to realize she should not to get friendly? Living next to such flamboyant gay men and hearing their loud antics could not have been any better. If this little girl did not grow up to make many errors I would surly be shocked.

That one incident is not the test by which I base my decision not to date women with children on. There is more than that incident. Like when I first arrived in California. It was early 1980s'. The hot trend of the day was wearing curls. I use to frequent one hair salon often. It was down the street form the Forum in Inglewood. I herd that Magic and other Los Angeles Lakers players got their haircut there.

The good thing about this salon was not the fact that I could see Magic and the other stars that frequented the place. I enjoyed all the beautiful Black ladies that would come there. I ate a plenty off the tree of drop-dead beauty at first. Soon I realized that beautiful women were a dime a dozen in Los Angeles. Most of them were void of substance.

When my regular hairdresser moved out to open her own salon, I followed gladly. When I first walked into her new place, I was taken by a most lovely flower. She was working on another guy's hair. While waiting my turn I could not help noticing how all the other men were hitting on her. She would always come up with a clever way to put them in their places.

Although it was her beauty that first struck me, it was her whit and professionalism that turned me on. I said nothing the whole time I was there. This was a major feet in itself since I love to talk. I was so taken by her that I didn't want to open my mouth and insert foot. When I left, I could not think of nothing else but her and the bad thing was I knew nothing of her but her name. Every guy that came in the salon asked her name that it became a song in my mind. Denise.

On my way home, I hated myself for not saying anything to her. At the same time I was glad I didn't say anything to make a fool of myself. Hours passed and all I could think of was Denise. Finally, I decided I had to do something. I didn't want to call and I didn't want to go right back. I knew all I would do is make a fool of myself. I went down to florist to send her some roses.

"Denise; I saw you and lost my voice for your beauty made impotence of my vocal cords. Your wit tantalized me. I knew not how to approach you. I know not if you are spoken for. All I know is that I needed to tell you how much you touched me." I wrote on a card.

I signed the card and put my phone number on it. I had the flowers sent and I waited. 5:00pm, she must just be getting the flowers. 5:30, she must still be working. 6:00 I guess she did not like the flowers. 6:30, maybe I should call the florist to see if they delivered the flowers. 7:00, she must be married. I didn't look to see if she was wearing a ring. 7:30, boy was that a dumb thing to do. I could never go back there again. 8:00, she calls.

Denise told me she received my flowers and was moved by my message. She told me she had no idea who I was. I explained that I was in the salon that day and was amazed by how she was able to put those men in their places. When she realized who I was, she asked why I did not say anything. She said I was noticeably quiet. She asked if I were shy. I told her about not wanting to put my foot in my mouth. This made her laugh.

We got together the next day for dinner. We hit it off pretty well. Denise had three children, a girl by her first husband, and two boys by her second husband. It was hard to imagine this attractive lady with a body of a dancer could have given birth to three kids. Denise was a member of the fool me twice club. Her justification was that at lease she was married to the fathers at the time.

Her children were very sweet. I felt like daddy. Every time I went over to her place, the children would jump all over me. It took the first child a while to warm up to me. She would sit by herself while the two boys jumped all over me. Finally, when she felt comfortable with me she joined in fray.

It became disturbingly clear to me I fell in love with the three children before I fell for Denise. Today I cannot remember if I ever kissed her. I know we never made love. We went out many times. I had the pleasure of getting to know her mother and sister but I do not remember ever getting to know Denise.

Here I was with clearly one of the most attractive ladies in Los Angeles and I'm thinking of her more as mother rather than a lover. When I began to realize this, I knew I had to end it. Those children weren't mine. I loved them very much but I didn't know their mom. Their fathers were very much a part of their lives too. This was another reason I had to let go. I was jealousy of their time with their fathers.

If there is any one event that molded my opinion of dating ladies with children, Denise was the event in my life I will never forget. Falling in love with the children before falling for their mother is very painful for me as well as the children. Denise was clearly a beautiful lady. She was witty, fun, and sexy. I overlooked all of that and only saw a mother.

First, I meet a lady whose need for a man outweighed her responsibility as a parent. Raising a child that knew to disappear whenever a man came around was unforgivable. Then I meet a lady whose children became more important to me than the lady herself did. The pain of leaving Denise was multiplied three times. My next experience was the most painful.

One Thanksgiving eve I was extremely horny. I had not had a date in months. I had gotten tired of trying so hard and falling short. I had become bitter about women. I was beginning to feel nice guys do finish last. That night I knew there were many of my Black ladies getting beat, cheated on, abused, and neglected by the men in their lives. Hear I was, a man more than willing to give a lady what they claim they wanted, sitting at home alone.

My bitterness was fueled by hearing my male friends brag about the women they had. These men all were married. My bitterness was fueled by walking the streets and seeing beautiful Black women with guys with their pants hanging off them. My anger was fueled by watching one lady at work come in at lease once a week with a bruise from her husband. That night I was going out to get laid. I was going to turn into a dog and treat women the way I thought they really wanted to be treated.

I got all dressed up and went to a nightclub by the house. There I met a lady that was dress up like a dime hooker. I did not care I just wanted what she had between her legs. She was wearing fish net stockings. She had on a leather skirt that was two sizes too small for all that butt she had in it. Her lips were two huge cowcatchers like on old fashion trains.

Figuring this was the prime candidate for my midnight game of in and out, I went up to her and asked her to dance. We danced a while, we drank a while, and we danced some more. I have to admit I enjoyed playing the dog role. I did not care at all about this lady. All I wanted to do was to make her think I liked her enough to get her in my bed, and it worked.

In the car while driving back to my place, I had my hand on her big thighs. I do not think I herd a word she said. All I knew was I could not drive fast enough. When we got to my place, I sat her down on the couch. I slid my hand up that short skirt I started rubbing her fur patch through her panties. I began kissing those cowcatchers. Then the worst thing that could happen, happened. I got a conscience.

I pulled my hand away from her soaked panties, kissed her on the cheek and pulled away.

"What's the matter baby? Don't I turn you on?" she questioned.

"That's not it." I went on; I just can't do this like this. We are moving too fast don't you think?"

"You think I'm ugly don't you? I know that's what you thinking. You think I'm a dog!"

If you can imagine Wanda on **"In Living Colors"**, this was her. Only this Wanda was not being played by a man. Still I could not tell her this.

"No baby you're not a dog at all. I just cannot dog you out this way. It's not in me to be a dog."

"Come on baby, all Black men are dogs, I know that. I just want me an obedient hound."

"You should be looking for a king, not some dog named King. All men aren't dogs. If you look hard enough you'll find your king."

"Will you be my king? That is if you don't think I'm too ugly to be your queen."

It became obvious to me this lady was suffering from a bad case of low self-esteem. I knew I couldn't be her king; she was too God-awful ugly for me. Still I couldn't dog her either. We talked for a while and I took her home.

By the time I returned home, she had called and left a message for me to call her back when I got in. When I called, she asked me to come back over. She planed to be up all night to prepare Thanksgiving dinner for her children. Out of guilt for what I was going to do to this lady, mixed with sympathy for her self-doubt and loneliness, I agreed to go back over to her house.

Ceecee as it turned out to be her name wasn't a bad person. She had her own childcare business. She had her own home and was sweet to talk to. She would not have been so ugly had she not tried so hard to look sexy. By trying to look sexy, she made herself look worse. That night after she took off those whore like cloths, and put on a robe, after she took off all that make-up especially that bright red lipstick, she didn't look that bad.

We talked while she cooked. When I got sleepy, she escorted me to her bedroom. Her bedroom looked like a little girls room with stuffed animals and glass figurines everywhere. The room was as sweet looking as she was sweet. I laid down and fell asleep. I remember she jointed me later in the night. She laid down next to me and fell asleep with her arm across my chest.

I was woken suddenly the next morning by such a racket that I thought there was a riot in the next room. I put my cloths on and went to see what was going on. Ceecee was in the kitchen cooking and there were five small children running around destroying the place. I went into the kitchen where Ceecee was and sat down at the table. Ceecee immediately sat a plate of pancakes and sausage down in front of me.

I asked if all the kids were hers. She began to explain that the children were hers. Two by one man, two by another man, and the last by yet another man. Ceecee told me the last man demanded she had one more child by him, because he refused to be the only man that gave her one baby. At his request, rather than to kick him out of her life, she went and had her tubes tied. She was tired of having babies.

I couldn't help but to feel sorry for Ceecee. She did not feel like she was in bad shape. Her low self-esteem allowed her to feel comfortable living this way. I still felt sorry for her. If Denise belonged to the "fool me twice club," then Ceecee was its CEO. After I ate the breakfast Ceecee prepared for me, I left to go to my mother's for Thanksgiving dinner.

I was never so thankful for what I had. I was even more thankful for what I did not have. I was thankful for not having fathered a child in that manner. Thankful for not having followed though on what my plan was the previous night. I was thankful for not having such a low opinion of myself.

Why I don't date women with children? Well I guess you can see why. I will continue to wait until I find that special lady that averted the mistakes many make and often regret. I will wait for the right lady to come along before I will vow, until death do us part. I am not sitting in judgment; I just cannot bare the pain.

"Forbear to judge, for we are sinners all."

—*Shakespeare.*

REFLECTIONS
ARE YOUR DESIRES
GREATER THAN YOUR
DIGNITY

you allow yourself to be misused by him
your partnership with your man is a daily battle
you concede to having illegitimate children
your reproduction is a small way of keeping him around
you succumb to beatings, and verbal abuse
your submission allows him power to stay with you
you suffer from his insatiable appetite for women
your monogamous belief is compromised as you knowingly share
you choose the ones that hurt you the most
your mind claims there aren't any better alternatives
you fear the solace of being alone
your dignity gives way to your fears and desires

REFLECTIONS
BEAUTY ALONE IN
YOUR TOILS

In the morning as I'm on my way to work, I see you on the corners waiting for the bus. I observe you walking down the streets in the cold morning air. I see you in your cars. As I watch, I notice how well you are dressed, you look ravishing, with every essence of you meticulously in place. Every morning as I see your enchantment, I can't help but to admire and desire you. You create a pride in me resulting in my joy to be an African American man who has to distinction of having the most beautiful women in the macrocosm.

My thoughts wonder as to what kind of day you have had already, so early, and I wonder what is yet to befall you. Did you leave home with your man still in bed? Did you have to get up early to prepare and to chauffeur your children to school? What kinds of altercation did you go through before you were able to be on your way, And just where is it you are going?

Are you off to school to cultivate your talents in order to possess a better existence, is your destination a job in which you need to feed yourself and your children, or are you off to a career that occupies your time and stimulates your need for the spotlight you are not getting personally?

There is one thing that I notice wrong about this picture. Where are my counterparts? My fellow brothers are noticeably missing from the arena of these early morning dramatics.

The drama unfolds to reveal the saga of disgrace as the morning gives way to afternoon. The unfortunate thing to see while driving through our communities as the noon hour unfolds, is the players now are my African American brothers. They are walking the streets, hanging out at the local liquor stores, and driving around with no specific destination.

The "home boys are kicking it," enjoying the afternoon sun or chasing after some trashy woman, while the beautiful ones, (our ladies,) are somewhere enriching themselves for us.

As you are on your way home from your protracted day, you have to further put up with our insensitive belittlement. You are castigated by sexual ploys from us on the streets. Our conceit surrenders to our conviction that, you, after spending your day feeding your children, preparing for work, rushing your children off to school, and putting in a long arduous day, you have nothing on your mind but to jump into bed with a sloppy, drunken, and disgusting man. You must be ashamed of us for what we represent.

You now have to spend time at home working as a homemaker, which is not an easy task in itself. The lucky ones of you do not have a lazy man in the home demanding his meal, and after eating, he demands you satisfy his sexual needs. Many of you have to clean house, feed your children, put up with drugs and crime crowding your doorway. Far too many of my lovely African American ladies have this burden to put up with every day, and you have to do it all alone.

CHAPTER FOUR
STRIKE TWO

Robert Hall once wrote:

"The wheels of nature are not made to roll backward; everything presses on toward eternity."

Just like the wheels of nature I too was not made to roll backwards, I had to press on. I knew she was out there somewhere. Where she was and how to find her was the $64,000.00 question. The odds were she was just like me. She worked, went to school, and came home to hug a sandwich while sitting in front of the television.

If I were to give up looking for her, I know I would end up settling for less than I feel I deserve. By settling, I might as well give up on life itself. I have seen too many people, even friends; give in to their painful loneliness, that they made choices only to have regrets.

I had received a letter in the mail to join a national dating service. The first correspondence was a questionnaire. Upon filling out the questionnaire and sending it in I was called to come down and touring the office. I had a choice of locations to visit. I chose the closest office to my home and made an appointment.

I was greeted at the office by a white lady who was going to be my tour guide. I mention her color because the next hour and a half was an evident education in race relations. First, she escorted me to a small cubical where I had to sit for twenty minuets and watch a brainwashing infomercial developed by the founder of this dating company. It obviously was a timed program because the second it was done my guide came back.

Next, she showed me a sitting room where clients would come and view the picture records and bios of the other clients who wanted to be matched. I was already skeptical about this place when I was first forced to sit alone in that cubical. When I saw the people that were sitting in that room, I became more skeptical. It was all men say for one woman. All the people were white and looked to be the type of people who couldn't buy a date if they had to.

Keep in mind I was told all though out this whole process that this was a classy and professional way to meet people. From the picture books, or wish books I thought in my mind, you went to a video room to view the video tapes in private of the people you chose. After showing me the video room and explaining how they professionally take your photo, and make your video tape, my escort then led me to the front message center where I would leave or pick up any messages from connections.

At this dating service, as it may be at all services, you only make contact after both parties have the opportunity to view each other's bios and video tapes. After showing me to entire operation my escort took me back to the library of photos. She grabbed one of the albums and flipped through the book until she found a picture of a Black lady. She told me this was the type of woman I would have to pick from.

My escort had such a huge smile on her face as if she had won the lottery. The lady she had picked was an extremely attractive and appealing lady. My escort was happy to have found such a specimen to display before me. Then her smile disappeared quickly when she read the bio. It turned out that my beautiful Black queen was looking for a white man.

"Oh my heavens!" She exclaimed. 'She is looking for a white man. Why is she seeking a white man? Well sir you have at lease an Idea of the type of women you can chose. I'm sorry she's looking for a white man." With honest sorrow, she exclaimed.

I guess my escort was not aware of how California is the Mecca for Blacks who wish to run from their heritage. She did not consider thinking I might be looking for a white woman. Her embarrassment was greatly in view for picking the wrong token. As well rehearsed as this placed appeared, this was the first kink in their armor. She obviously didn't rehearse the clients in the book. I was, in fact, looking for a Black lady and this negligent faux pas added just another nail in the coffin.

Red as a beet my escort led me to her office to give me her sales pitch. All the way to her office, she felt the need to constantly apologize for my lost sister. In the office, my glowing escort turned into a tenacious salesperson. She closed her door and offered me a membership for $1,500.00.

'Keep in mind, not all of our Blacks want white men. I guess that one was an exception." She exclaimed.

I told her I wanted to think it over. The truth was I was insulted and disgusted with this organization. She sat between me, the door, and the only way out was through her. She would not let me leave. She told me the real membership price was $2,500.00 per year and the only way to receive this price was by a one time offer after being personally walked through the vacillates. If I didn't buy now, I would pay the full amount. Again, I told her I had to think about it.

Without taking a breath, she went on to tell me what I was going to get for my $1,500.00. A professional sitting at a real photo studio and having professionally touched up photos to display with my bio. I would have a staff psychotherapist help me develop my bio. I would be videotaped at a professional location. Finally, I would be on line for an entire year. If I hadn't found a wife in a year, I would only pay $750.00 each year after. Again, I told her I really had to think it over. **She wouldn't let me leave.**

Next, she offered me a membership for $1,100.00. With that, I would get everything she mentioned except I would get a Polaroid instead of a professional shooting. Again, I said no and again she kept going. She then offered me membership for $750.00 if I were to bring in my own photos and video providing I felt I could have it done professionally and cheaper.

Then I started to get mad. I told her I needed to think it over at home and would call back with my answer. Still she would not let me go; instead, she told me to wait a minuet and left the room.

I didn't want to be rude but I was getting tired of the strong-arm antics. After she left the room, I was tempted to get up and leave. At best, I wanted to check the door to see if she locked it on her way out. I didn't leave because I was somewhat curious to see what was next. I do regret I never checked the door. Somehow, I believe she did lock it.

After sweating it out for five minuets, the second waive came in to continue the assault. This straw broke the camels back. The lady that was sent in to get me was a very attractive Black lady. She came in and asked me if I were having any trouble with the other lady. I told her no. She then asked if I had any questions to ask her about my membership. I told her that I just need time to think over the offer. I explained I never make huge purchases without much thought. In my mind, I was furious. To use a Black lady and think I might buy from her was an insult.

My lovely Black sister then gave me what they must have thought was the offer I could not refuse. For only five $500.00, I could go six months with full privileges and see how I might like the service. I repeated myself. I just want to think this over. I'm not looking for any kind of deal. Just give me time and I will let you know."

Feeling she had exhausted all their efforts of giving me such a *"special deal,"* my lovely Nubian queen then went for the jugular.

"You really aren't looking for a wife are you? You came here to waist our time. If you were looking for a wife, you wouldn't, no you couldn't pass up this offer. What I offered you was something unheard of. It was because I felt you were patient and because we have something in common that I offered you this. Maybe you aren't serious about finding someone." She attacked.

At that point, my anger flared up but she wouldn't let me get a word in edgewise. "Now come on, if you want to find a good quality woman this is the way to find her. A man of your caliber knows how difficult it is to find someone. If you were successful to this point, you would not have come here. $500.00 is not a lot of money to a man like you so why don't you go ahead and say yes. If you leave and call back, you will have to pay full price. This offer in only good right now. What do you say?"

Finally, she shut up! I was so angry and felt so insulted that it took a while for me to get my thought together, I was afraid of what I might say. "I'm not here to buy a used car," I went on to say. "Those tactics don't work on me at a car dealer and they won't work on me here. I am disgusted with the insults you have thrown at me and with not even knowing me. I am insulted with the quite little way you were sent in here to get me to buy. Did you think that I was that desperate not to see through this racial ploy of yours.

I think you should be ashamed of yourself. What are you anyway, their little Black girl to parade in front of Black men? You all have set a bad taste in my mouth. I suddenly feel, right now, that this place is nothing more than a prostituting cult for lonely hart's. All I asked was to have time to think it over. I have no problem paying your prices. If I chose to join I assure you it will be in spite of you not because of you!" I then got up and left.

The next day I received a phone call from yet another woman from that dating service. She apologized for what happen and tried to make an offer. I told her no and immediately hung up the phone. It was apparent to me that dating services, or at lease this one, was not an avenue I wanted to try. After all, I had better luck with personal ads, so I decided to try it again. This time I was going to be more descriptive.

Seeking Soul mate:

SBM 34 seeks SBF age 31-35, if you're tired of kissing frogs and getting warts and finding yourself dancing with wolves, if you have no children and tired of games, give me a try.

I also left a detailed phone recording. My last ad I didn't give an age range and I talked more about myself on the phone recording rather than telling what I was looking for. This time I did not want to make the same mistake. I wanted there to be no mistake as to what I was looking for.

"Hi, I'm a thirty three year old single Black man. I am very Afro centric, therefore I only want a Black lady. I am looking for someone between the ages of thirty-one and thirty-five. I have never been married nor do I have any children. I would like only to find someone who is in the same boat. You must have never been married nor have children. I am very health conscious and would like someone of the same. I am not looking for a bed partner or an adversary. That is easy to find out there in the streets. Gold diggers and game players need not to reply. If that is you, leave me a phone number and the best time to reach you."

This time I felt I was explicit enough that I surely would find a good match. I also choose a different paper to go into. This paper was the kind you had to look for. It was a trendy paper that advertised all the events that were happening in the city. The first paper was a throw away that came to everyone's homes. I figured a different kind of person would be looking at this paper. This paper also ran the ad longer. I would have my ad running for five weeks every Thursday.

Maybe my phone message was too explicit or maybe the paper was too exclusive. The first two weeks I checked for messages only to find no one had responded. I was greatly discouraged. I began to think that the lady I was looking for did not exist. On the third week when I didn't get a response, I out of desperation looked through ads and decided to respond to a few myself. Up to that point it never dawned on me to respond to someone else ad.

I had in the past looked at personal ads for entertainment value. It wasn't until I had placed one myself; I considered them as anything less. One thing that always intruded me as well angered me was that without exception every Black man was looking for white women. I would always see: SBM looking for SWF, SHF, or SAF. I would almost never see: SBM looking for SBF. The reverse was true of my Black ladies. I hardly saw a Black lady looking for anything else but a Black man.

Through the years, I noticed a great change in personals. Today you find Black men are seeking SF. This must be because many of my sisters must have called the ads of those betrayers and read them the riot act. So now Black men use the generic SF to mean SWF, SHF, and SAF. If a Black lady calls, he would not respond back. What is most disturbing is how my Black women now seek white men unlike they have in the past.

In any case, at that time, I did find two ads that peeked my curiosity. The first was from a lady who also asked for no children. The second was a lady that ran a straightforward ad. I would rule out all the ads that would state *"bubbling brown sugar," "Sexy chocolate dream," or "long lushes legs."* Somehow those kind of catch phrases were turn offs to me.

When the first lady called me back, we had a very combative conversation. It was not that we were fighting; it was more as if I had a problem with her line of questioning. First, she asked;

"What kind of car do you have?"

Feeling this was more a question to find out the worth of a person than anything else was, I took offence of the question.

"That's an interesting question. Why do you ask?" I responded.

She told me she asked only to see if I had a car. "I meet so many men that expect me to drive because they don't have a car. I'm tired of low lives that still live at home and expect me to do everything."

I asked why she didn't ask if I had a car instead. She offered that it was because she found that the best way to find out if I had one. I told her I had a car but didn't tell her what kind.

"Well OK," she responded. "Let me as you this. Do you live with mamma?"

"No, I live alone."

"Good, do you live in an apartment or a house?"

Again, a red flag was raised. Why on earth would she be asking that unless she was digging? Thinking she was not going to strike gold here, I asked why she asked that question.

"I'm just trying to get to know who you are. You are taking everything too personal." She exclaimed.

"Well if you are trying to get to know me, I guess that means you want to know the person. Why wouldn't I take such personal questions personally?" I replied.

"OK I see you want to be difficult. I will assume that since you are having such a hard time answering my questions, you must have a BMW or something like that and you must live in a mansion. Let's change the subject. Describe yourself?" she said with great sarcasm.

"Well I'm 6' 3" tall. I weight about 215lbs. I have short hair and a mustache. I would say I'm pretty average." I responded

"That's no help. I need to envision you. Give me more than that. Tell me who do you look like?" she exclaimed.

Once again, she was treading in an area I was not happy to be visiting.

"What do you mean?" I asked, knowing what she was driving at.

"Come on you know what I mean. People say I look like Vanessa Williams a little. Who do people say you look like?" Again, she said with a sarcastic tone.

"Most people I know say I look like my father. I don't think that would be much help to you." Sarcastically I responded.

"Ha, Ha, very funny, I bet you thought that was quite."

"No. I wasn't trying to be quite, just honest. I do not idolize stars so I have no interest in trying to look like anybody but me. Is that so bad?" I asked.

"You really are going to be difficult. Let's try this question. I know you will try to find something about it to be difficult about, but let me try anyway. What color are you?" She went there and to my surprise.

"I'm Black! Couldn't you tell?" I replied. I knew just what she was looking for but I decided to be difficult after all.

"Don't be silly, of course I knew you were black. I mean what color are you. Are you light skinned or dark skinned?" She came back with.

"Does it matter? I'm Black like you that's all that should matter."

"I knew you would find a reason to make this difficult. Are you yellow light skinned like a banana, or are you light like a paper bag? Are you brown like coco, mahogany, or brown like tree bark? Are you dark as dark chocolate or jet black?"

At that point, I could not take anymore. I told this lady it was obvious we did not have anything in common. I explained I was not comfortable with the direction of conversation. I had enough and said good-buy to her. After that call, it took me a while to come down from it. I couldn't believe what kind person that was to ask those questions. If she wanted a man that could comfortably answer questions like that, then I wish her luck.

The other lady whose ad I responded to never called me. I was glad in a sense. After the experience I had talking to that last one, I was beginning to think my first impressions of personal ads were correct. I had my share of sexual degenerates, social misfits, gold diggers, and freaks. I was ready to throw in the towel. I decided to just throw myself into my work.

At the end of the fifth week of my ad, I decided to check if I received any responses. I wasn't really interested but I have to admit my loneliness was getting the best of me. I hoped that somehow God would direct my soul mate to me. No matter how much I buried myself in my work I couldn't help feeling lonely.

There was only one response on my message line. I could hardly make out the voice. She talked so softly. Her name was Patrice. She said she was thirty-four years old, never married, no children and was very interested and impressed with my phone message.

I called Patrice right away. The first thing she asked was if what I meant by having no children was that I didn't know if I had any or was it that I didn't claim any. I thought this was cute. I have herd many men make those statements. I relayed to her that I was responsible for my seeds and knew where everyone was. I knew I never father a child and would never one until I was married.

With that Patrice asked if we could meet right then. I was set back a little. I never imagined I would meet someone after only twenty minuets of talking on the phone. Something told me to take the chance and go. I did not get a chance to get a good feeling or a bad feeling about Patrice. We agreed to meet a bar not too far from my house.

When I arrived at the bar, I was pleasantly surprised by what I saw. Patrice was 5'7" tall. She had the longest legs I had ever seen. She wore her hair in a short style that accentuated her face just right. The kicker was she wore glasses. Very few people know I am turned on by ladies who wear glasses. By all design, Patrice was what I would have in my mind as the perfect lady. I was sure that someone who wanted to meet so fast would be two tons of perverted fun. Patrice was far from that.

After talking for a while, I began to feel Patrice had a good chance of being her, Ms. Right. With all the bad luck I have had, I was extremely cautious about jumping to conclusions. The adage, if it sound too good to be true, it is, kept whistling through my mind. With every word Patrice spoke, I kept saying, this is too good to be true.

Over the next couple of days, Patrice and I talked on the phone. We had so much in common. Our views on things were almost alike. Our family background was also similar. It was too good to be true. I wanted to make sure Patrice was not like the other disappointments I had suffered through. By this time, I had developed practices that would ensue protection. There for I had not told Patrice where I lived. She didn't know what kind of car I drove and I did not tell her what I did. She never pushed for that information either.

I happen to like old cars, and part of my collection was an old 1960 Ford Ranchero. I had not yet restored it and it made a good first date car. My sister would always make fun of that car. She thought it was a piece of junk. This made it perfect for my purpose. By the time it came to have my first date with Patrice, I drove the Ranchero.

The first date went without a hitch. Patrice never said anything about my car; we just enjoyed each other as we did when we first met. We went to a movie and from there we went to a park. It was spooky how we enjoyed the same things. One thing I love to do is swing on the swings at a playground. Patrice and I did that on our first date. This was too good to be true.

We spent good quality time together when we did. We would go on picnics, see movies, or go to the park. She would even cook me dinner at times. Every time we would be together, I drove my beat up Ranchero or rode my motorcycle. Still I did not let on as to where I lived. I might have been too cautious and guilty of plying a game, but this was too good to be true. She was too perfect.

I had, at the time, a very close group of friends. We all worked in the same field and because of the demands of the job, found it difficult to have a life away from the job. That is how we became so close. We worked twelve plus hours a day together. Most people who work in this field are divorce or alone because spouses and/or significant others do not seem to understand the hours we put in. We weren't doctors, police, or firemen so why did we put in so many hours?

In this group were three guys along with me, and five ladies. We ranged in age and color. We had the greatest times together. We organized sky trips, runs to Las Vegas, but mostly we spent time together twice a week or more at a local happy hour just to talk and relieve each other. It was often rumored that one of the guys were sleeping with one of the ladies, but it ever happened. There were clicks among us but as a group, we stayed together for a long time.

One of the ladies in this group was the one that introduced me to personal ads. I thought it only fitting that I introduce her to Patrice. That is how serious it was getting between Patrice and me. Seldom did anyone bring their spouses or significant other into the group. Here I was ready to introduce her to my extended family. I only took her once to meet everybody. She had a good time because we had a habit of leaving all inhibitions checked at the door.

We were two months into knowing each other before I stopped saying it were too good to be true. By then I felt comfortable in bringing her to my home. I stopped playing the car game and she never questioned it. I made her dinner many times because I love to cook for people. We were headed in the right direction. There was one thing that bothered me. Making love to Patrice was an experience.

The first time Patrice and I made love, everything was as normal as it could get. I loved Patrice's legs. I couldn't make love to her without spending a lot of time enjoying her long beautiful soft juicy legs. We made love often and in many positions. The curious ingredient she added to our lovemaking happened just before she had an orgasm. Her eyes would go back and she would start going into convulsions.

The first time this happened I jumped off her scared that she was about to die of something. I just looked at her waiting to see if I had to call an ambulance. Patrice's eyes came back forward and she looked up at me and asked what was wrong, why did I stop. She told me she was about to cum. I couldn't believe what I just saw. She frightened the pants off me, that is if I had pants on.

Nervously I told Patrice what I saw. I did not know if this was normal for her or not but it made me nervous. Patrice began to laugh. At that moment, I knew she was crazy. She laughed and assured me that it was normal. She went on to apologize for not warning me ahead of time. Patrice continued to explain that she really enjoys lovemaking and has extreme reactions to having orgasms. She told me that she seldom has those kinds of orgasms the first time she is with a man. That is why she didn't warn me. She further warned me that I haven't experienced the worst of it yet.

We went back to making love and the next time she came close to cuming I was ready. Back went her eyes and again she went into convulsions. I continued to give it to her. The more I trusted the more violent her convulsions got, when finally she let out the strangest noise. Suddenly I felt I was in the middle of a Zulu war dance. Patrice started making the strangest sounds. The Only way to enplane it is to say it sounded like a Zulu war call. Then Patrice started talking in the strangest language that I couldn't make out. She would gradually calm down, her eyes would come back to the front and she was fine.

This was by far the strangest sexual experience I had ever had. I couldn't tell if I were killing her or if she was possessed by some kind of demon. It took me a while to feel comfortable with making love to Patrice. Once I did, I really got a kick out of it.

Everything was going along find for months. I had been introduced to Patrice's family. Her mother was a bit on the fringes. She was more like a cool creature of life than a stiff mother type. Patrice had two brothers one older and one younger. The older one was married to an Asian woman he met in the Philippians while in the service. The younger brother only dated Hispanic women. Patrice had an older sister who was very religious.

I don't know if Patrice and her sister had a difficult relationship but I felt there had to be something there. Patrice would often accuse me of liking her sister. I don't know where this was coming from, but I didn't want to fuel it. Her sister had a very mysterious quality about her, but to me Patrice had more going for her than her sister did. I remember once talking about to Patrice about the mystery of her sister. That must have been why she had those feelings of jealousy.

Patrice also had an aunt that was an older version of Patrice. If I were to carry a torch for anyone, it would have been her aunt. Like Patrice's mother, her aunt carried an air of not taking life too serious. I remember we were at a party once and both Patrice's mother and aunt fit in more with the people our age than with people their own age.

I felt so good about Patrice that I took her to meet my mother. Prior to Patrice my mother only met maybe three or four of the ladies in my life. I never wanted my mom to meet anyone unless I was serious about the person. Patrice was someone I was serious about even if we had only been seeing each other for four months.

At some point in the fifth month of our relationship, I bought a telephone answering machine. Until that time, I never liked them. I always felt that I couldn't miss a call I wasn't there to answer anyway. After falling for Patrice, I soon realized I didn't want to take any calls unless they were from her. With an answering machine, I could screen calls. If the call was from work, I did not have to answer. This gave me time to be with Patrice. Prior to getting the answering machine, I might be called to work and have to cancel a date with her.

Often I would return home from work to find that Patrice left me a message to hear upon my return. This was a cute and much appreciated message to hear at the end of my day. Often I would hear a strange message. It was a number of beeps. I did not think much about it at first. This went on for a month before I figured out what it was.

One day while at work Patrice was kind enough to have a dozen roses sent to me. I had never had anyone send me flowers before. I had sent them myself, but never received any. This was just another of the things Patrice would do to make me feel loved. I had always thought I would be embarrassed to receive such a gesture. On this occasion, I was very pleased. At the end of my workday, I could not wait to get home to hear Patrice's message that I called and retrieved it from work.

Driving home that night with the flowers in my car, I couldn't wait to call Patrice. My day was extended longer than I had planed and I was running a little late. By the time I got home and checked my messages, I found that Patrice had already called. I herd her first message that I had picked up from work, then I herd those beeps again, and finally I herd her second message to call her when I got home.

When I immediately called her back, I was stricken by the strangest realization. Those beeps! When I called from work to pick up Patrice's message that was the first time I had used that function. I realized those beeps came between her first call and her second call. When I got off the phone with her, I couldn't shake the terrible thought I had.

The next day the first thing I did was to call myself and leave a message. After hanging up I redialed to retrieve the message. That whole day I could not wait to get home to disprove what I was thinking. When I got home, I was devastated by my findings. There was my message first followed by those beeps. There were two more messages followed by those beeps then finally Patrice's daily message.

The code to my answering machine was posted under the lid of the machine. There were only two people to have been in my house that could have seen the code. Patrice was one and my mother was the other. I could not bring myself to ask Patrice if she had been retrieving my personal phone calls. I called my mother. Knowing it was not her, I asked her anyway.

Still not able to bring myself to ask Patrice if it were she, I concocted a plan to find out. If it was her, I couldn't think of what I would do if I found that out. Patrice and I had planed to take a trip to San Francisco the next week. I asked my mother to come over after we were gone to switch answering machines.

I could not enjoy myself in San Francisco. All the time I was wondering if this lady was so devious that she would steal my privacy in such a corrupt way. Patrice kept asking me what was wrong the whole time we were there. I had to constantly make up reasons for my distance. By the time we got home Thursday night, I couldn't wait to see what she was going to do.

Ironically, the first thing she had to do was use the phone when we got back. My mother had switched the machines and she would have to see that they were switched. I felt like a character from a Sam Spade novel as I tried to not be obvious in looking at her use the phone. Very much like a cool temptress from the same novel, Patrice showed no signs of being nervous about the change. She spent the night and went home the next day, Friday, as if nothing was different.

I was beginning to think that maybe it was not her. After all, she didn't act guilty at all. I called my mother and told her nothing happened. That night I did not call Patrice because I was so embarrassed about what I obviously was wrong about. I did not realize until I went to bed that she hadn't called me either. This was strange.

Saturday I decided to wait for Patrice to call. I thought it strange of her not to have called Friday. All day Saturday, I waited. No call. Sunday the same thing. I didn't hear from Patrice all day. By the end of Sunday night, I decided to call Patrice and put an end to my suspicions.

Monday morning when I went out to work there was a letter at my front door. The letter was from Patrice and it read like a classic case of delusional paranoid schizophrenia. The letter had no clear understanding. She called me every name in the book, from laying sack of shit, to demented fucking bastard.

She went on to state; I was going to die a broken rich lonely motherfucker who will only have my money to warm me at night in the Hearst castle. As I read Patrice's letter I could not help to think she was a sick confused soul. I could not make any connections to anything she was ranting about in her letter. Confused I went to work. All day I tried to make the connections in Patrice's letter. She made no sense. The only thing that had changed since coming home from San Francisco was my answering machine.

The next twist to this fatal attraction occurred at work. I received a call from Barbara. Barbara was a friend in my extended family group. Barbara told me she had lunch with Patrice on Sunday. This came as a complete shock to me. Patrice had only met my friends once over a month earlier. It turned out she had tracked Barbara down by knowing which company we all worked for that Friday.

Barbara told me that Patrice had come to her job Friday and offered to by lunch. At lunch, she asked a multitude of questions about me personally. When I asked why Patrice went to her, Barbara told me that Patrice said we were having trouble and I would not talk. Patrice stated she might be able to get more out of Barbara first. Shocked and amazed at what Barbara was telling me I listened while Barbara told me that on Sunday, she had Patrice over to her house and they talked more.

I then got angry a Barbara. I asked why she did not call me first before talking to Patrice. I told her I thought we were friends. Barbara told me that she care for me and wanted Patrice to understand that I needed space. Barbara told Patrice that since she didn't really know what our problem was it would be best that Patrice left me alone and I would appreciate that.

Suddenly I was now able to understand what Patrice's' letter meant. Over the years, Barbara and I grew very close. I considered her my best friend. We constantly had one thing that stood in the way of our friendship. She had a major crush on me. I thought of Barbara only as a good friend. Barbara always wanted more. I remember once, one of the other guys in our group told me that Barbara once told him; AI would gladly hand him my pussy on a silver platter. The only thing is he would not take it." She said this about me.

Barbara resented the fact that I enjoyed spending time with Patrice. I had often canceled out on going to our get nights out in order to be with Patrice. Barbara was a drinker. She enjoyed getting drunk. I did not like that one thing about her. She also was a bit overweight for my taste. That is why we never connected. Barbara knew why I was not attracted to her. She had asked me once if her weight was the problem. I did not want to tell her yes and although I tried to use another excuse, she knew the truth. Barbara always called Patrice, "***Ms. Perfect Body,***" when referring to her.

Two and Two was beginning to add up to four. The only thing I could justify was that Patrice, seeing the answering machine had changed felt like she had been busted. The fact I didn't say anything about it caused her guilt to escalate into lunacy. She tried to find a way to get close to me that she went to a friend of mine. It doesn't make sense but if fitted.

The pieces of the puzzle were coming more together when I talked to my mother. My mother also called me at work that Monday. It was rare for my mother to call me at work so I thought something was wrong. The first thing out of her mouth was how things are going with Patrice and me. Suspiciously, I asked why she asked. My mother told me that Patrice called her Saturday and offered to take her to an African Arts Fair. My mother being a little more intelligent that Barbara declined. She didn't know I had no knowledge of this. I filled my mom in on the events. To that point, we both were confused and in agreement, That Patrice was the one checking my phone messages. This could only be the reason she was acting so strangely. She felt trapped. We also figured Patrice was on the hunt for that answering machine.

When I arrived home that Monday I still intended to call Patrice as planed but I was met by a phone message the curled the hair on my back. I was the ravings of a mad woman, and it was Patrice. I called her up and asked her to come over. I felt bad for playing a trick on her. I wanted her to tell me she was the one checking my messages and I would forgive her. I realized the other ranting was because Barbara had put strange ideas in her head.

Patrice came over and I didn't know who she was. She looked like a possessed witch. Her hair was all array, her cloths looked like she had been sleeping in them, and she had the strangest glare in her eyes. I asked Patrice what was going on. Why did she not call me if she thought there was a problem? Why did she write the letter? Why did she hunt down a friend of mine? Why did she call my mother? I asked her why all these events went down right after we had spent a fine time in San Francisco. I told her that the only thing that changed in our relationship was my answering machine. I still didn't want to straight out accuse her of checking my calls without proof. I thought she might take the hint a run with it.

She didn't take the hint. She just went on to tell me that she wanted to know more about me and thought my family and friends might give her an insight I would not give. I explained to Patrice that what she did was an act of backstabbing betrayal. I told her that she should have come to me first if she wanted to see my friends or family. I told her that Barbara was my best friend but what Patrice didn't know was that she had a crush on me. Nothing that Barbara might tell her would be offered in friendship rather that it would be offered to break us up. I offered again that she should have come to me. The only thing that changed was the answering machine.

Again, Patrice didn't take the bait. Either she chose to disregard what I was saying or she didn't want to confess, never the less I was willing to forget what had happened. Despite the craziness expounded in her letter, in spite of the back stabbing meetings, I was willing to try again because I cared a great deal for Patrice. I asked her to promise me that she would come to me first if she felt something was wrong. She agreed and we left it at that. I had not found out if she was the spy but I was willing to let it go.

Two days latter, I get another disturbing phone message when I came in from work. Again, Patrice was ranting and raving about me being a fucking lair. She stated she wanted to come over and cut my balls off. This time when I called Patrice, I had had enough. I asked her what the problem was this time. She told me she just left Barbara and Barbara told her the real truth. When I questioned Patrice why she didn't come to me like we agreed, she told me that Barbara was her friend and she didn't feel the need to ask my permission to visit a friend. I reiterated that Barbara was not her friend. That she had divergent motives. Fed up I, told Patrice I had enough and that we were through.

Over the next month, I was called constantly by Patrice leaving disturbing messages. Once she told me to go and turn the tape into the police because I would be dead before they would have time to do anything. She would follow me around as if stalking me. That movie kept flashing in my mind that I thought one day I would come home to find my cat boiling in a pot.

Thank goodness, Patrice's threats never happened. After a month of harassment and stalking Patrice finally ended her constant attacks. I never saw her again but once two years latter at an African Expo. I was going in and she was coming out. We looked in each other's direction but never made eye contact or spoke. I spoke to Barbara only once after that incident. That too was two years later. Barbara had gone through a nervous brake down after loosing her job. Regrettably, I thought of Gods justice. Maybe God had punished Barbara for the mental anguish she inflicted on Patrice.

REFLECTIONS
I'M A MAN DAMMIT!

What's up with all this damn fuss about Black men not being strong enough, or not having enough pride and desire to fucking succeed? Do you think I want to be selling fucking drugs? Do you think I want to be in a fucking gang? My wakening thoughts are not aimed at the next victim I can do over. I'm a man dammit, and I want to be treated like a man. I want the fucking respect that a man is supposed to get.

You fucking tell me how I'm going to get respect, when from the time I'm born, I'm considered less than human by the system, and what a fucking system. My mama did her best raising me by herself because my old man didn't care enough for her to stick around. I'm put into an educational system that cares more about controlling the damn person than growing a mind. I learn to fight before I learn to read. I learn to steel before I learn to care. The damn football coach is turning out the whole cheer leading squad, and sex, drugs and guns are part of my real fucking education.

The reality I'm fucking learning in school is further enforced by what I see on television. I see Dynasty and Dallas where all these lily boys making much money and having much power that I will never fucking have. Life is fucking great as long as you have white fucking skin. What do you get if your skin is darker? You get a fucking jail cell.

You have to be a fucking Michael Jordan or Michael Jackson to be successful, if you are not; you become a damn garbage man, and know one wants to be bothered with you. As I said this system, fucking sucks.

Then you have enough nerve to fucking criticize me of being a weak man. Until you can live your life in my shoes don't make any judgments. I have damn pride, I'm fucking strong enough. I'm fucking lucky to be alive right now. From the time I could talk, life has been a fucking battle. Mama never had enough money to give me what I needed, so I learned how to get for myself.

I have a pride, I am a fucking man, I don't need anybody doing for me when I can do for myself. I learned who the best people to hang out with were. I learned how to get money; after all, that's what's important to every fucking body isn't it?

I would like to have one of those "cake," nine to five jobs that you see on TV, but as you see, they are for white boys or pansy ass white talking black fuckers. I'm not one of those, that's not for me. I'm from the ghetto, my homeboys and I come from the streets where we get over the old fashion way, we earn it with our blood. We pay our dues with a turn in jail. We fucking make it to the top just by surviving the war out there.

After all is said and done, I have to put up with my sisters telling me I not fucking good enough, what kind of shit is this? You bitches are living in La-La land if you think you are going to find a fucking white knight to sweep you off your feet. That kind of shit only happens in fairy tails, and you see the color of the faces in fairy tails.

You have a lot of fucking nerve saying we are not strong, or stating we have no dreams. I have dreams, big fucking dreams, but how can I accomplish them when the white man is out to keep me down. Every time I try to move up, he finds a way to put me down.

My first job, my boss gave the white boys all the brakes while making me do all the work. I was fucking treated like dirt, and I sure in hell was not going to stay there. The next job I had, there was this fucking Uncle Tom as the boss. He had it out for me. Here, I'm thinking this brother is a homeboy, and all the time he's telling the man on me trying to get me fired. I'm thinking what kind of shit is this; he should cut me some slack being from the hood and all. Needless to say I told him to fuck off and I went on my way.

At lease in the streets, you know what's what, and you can count on your homeboys. You can see the shit I have to put up with, so don't tell me I haven't any pride. Don't fucking tell me I have no dreams, I'm only playing with the hand this world fucking dealt me.

I can take care of my kids; I can take care of myself. I don't live in a world of delusions.

Maybe that is your problem. You are caught up in a fucking dream world. This is reality, you need to come back to earth and accept the reality that you won't be Cinderella. Sleeping beauty will never wake up because there is never going to be a prince charming.

You better learn to stop looking down your noise at me and start accepting me as I am. The problem with all you bitches is that you are looking for something you will never find. Get your ass out of the clouds and stand by your man. I'm a man dammit!

CHAPTER FIVE
GREAT EXPECTATIONS

Most people would enter into a period of anger after going through the experiences I'd suffered through. The most devout Christian, the most devoted Catholic, the most enlightened Buddhist, would go through the classic steps of depression. Sorrow, denial, and anger were the next steps. I was not saved that trip down psychobabble lane.

The statement from the movie Mahogany often would ring so loud in my head, when I would come home at the end of my day to an empty house that had nothing to offer me but a TV, and a cat for company. "**Success is nothing without someone to share it with.**" What did I really have to show for my time here on earth? Houses, cars, toys of every kind could not hug me when I was depressed. Those things could not comfort me when I was in need.

I became so sad that I couldn't bare watching two people kiss on TV. I couldn't stomach any form of love song to play on my radio. I became a junkie of talk radio because they don't play love songs. At my lowest moments, I was thankful not to have a gun in my house. I would have surely made pizza art on my walls with a little lead mixed with brain matter. I do not think I would have actually put a bullet in my skull, but I was afraid of having that option.

My mom, sister and I are pretty close, but they couldn't understand where I was coming from. Everyone has his or her own crosses to bear. Everyone speaks from the agenda of their own experiences. I was tired to hearing how I didn't need someone to qualify my life. I could do a lot better if I waited. This was great jargon, but not what I needed to, nor wanted to hear. My family is great support however; they could not replace the lonely void in my life.

My pain was so great that I would become emotional about littlest things. I once became very emotional after seeing the movie "**Forest Gump**," not because I felt for the character in the movie, but I saw myself as the idiot. I felt an idiot for wanting to be in love. I felt like an idiot because I missed getting up early Sunday morning with someone sleeping next to me. I felt like an idiot for having so much and yet so little. I was hurt deeply for feeling like such an idiot.

I had made a somewhat success of myself in my career. I had reached the glass ceiling and was making a living that gave me such great material goods to come home to. My stockings were filled but my hart was empty. After experiencing such a disasters love life, I became resentful of the things I had. Like King Midas, I learned having the golden touch was more hart aching than being poor and fed by love.

My sorrow turned into justification. I began to think God was punishing me for holding on to false idols. Maybe I was being punished for some hurt I caused along the way. Then I thought it was my destiny to be alone. I obviously had a different idea of love than everyone else had, so I was sent here to suffer and be an outcast while everyone else was happy.

I began to be a minister of love for my friends, coworkers and employees. Everyone called me preacher for the way I would always interject my beliefs on them. **"Go home and tell your wife you love her,"** was my favorite saying. I would tell many men how much I envied them for having someone to go home to. While most men envied my life of freedom and toys, I would remind them how lonely and empty my life was.

One of the reasons I enjoyed management was that I could make a difference. I molded some of the best employees. I'm extremely proud of many of my children. I called them my children because I cared so much about them. It became extremely rewarding when I realized they cared just as much for me.

One year during the fires in Los Angeles, my house was in the line of the fire. On that day, I received fifteen phone calls from what was at that time past and present employees. They all were concerned that I was all right. I felt like my children really cared for my well-being. That is when I realized I might have made a difference in their lives. As a manager, I always tried to develop my people both professionally and personally, so they could someday take over my position or become as successful as they wanted and I could move on.

Although my preaching helped some of the people I talked to, the void of my loneliness was too great. I remembered the phrase of physician heal thyself and was eventually thrown into a period of anger. I was tired of being alone. I was tired of feeling pity for myself. I was tired to others feeling sorry for me, that I became hostile.

My resentment for my achievements caused me to leave a job I was with for sixteen years. What good was it to rise to the higher levels of the corporate ladder only to suffer the gut wrenching voids it produced? I gave up my expense account, my five weeks of vacation, my national recognition, and my status. I did not want those things that defined me by what I was worth. My pain was eased for all of a day before I realized I was going to miss the many associations I made through the years. I was only running from myself not solving any problems.

My hostility grew by leaps and bounds, as I became angry with my Black sisters for putting me through such a painful existence. Many brothers talk about how there are so many woman in the world, five for every one man. All I wanted was one lady. I was angry that my ladies were willing to share men with other women rather than to live a life of devotion with me. To be thought of, as bitches and whores, like they are called in rap songs, is what I thought my ladies preferred. I began to think the obedient dog mentality was what my ladies wanted.

Loving and respecting my mother and sister as I do, and knowing what they have gone through as women, Black women, and Black lady dealing with my Black brothers, I realized my hatred and resentment for my Black queens was misguided. I began to harvest great and intense loathing of my Black Brothers. I, to this day, find it difficult to call a Black brother, friend. Just like the sentiment Seely expressed to Brother in "**The Color Purple**," my brothers should be cursed until they do right by their Black queens.

Dr. Martin Luther King Jr. once said that we should be judged not by the color of our skin but by the content of our character. What is the content of the character of a Brother that beats his lady? What value is the character of a Brother that makes babies and abandons both the baby and the lady? What is the character of a Brother that once becoming successful he abandons his heritage and his lady for a white woman?

There is a form of Black on Black crime that is not on the news. This most inauspicious act of self-genocide barely is examined. Our children see this crime in progress daily. This crime is not perpetrated against the bodies of Blacks. It severs the soul of Blacks. This crime annihilates more Black families and will devastate the race more than any drive-by.

In this crime, we seem as primitive as the wolf. When caught in a trap, the wolf will chew off his own leg to get free. Self hate and self-loathing is by far the worst injustice we inflict on our selves. Unlike the wolf, our trap is not from an external force but is a perceived internal confine. That trap is manifested in our skin. However just as the wolf, we are gnawing and tearing away a vital part of us to escape our perceived capture.

I have seen us make great gains in education, arts, and in the arena of sport. We sit on the highest court of the land. We have won recognition as outstanding artist. We have received Oscars, Grammies, and Tony's. We have impress the world with our outstanding ability to command monumental greatness if the field of sport. We have cured the sick, successfully debated the enigmas of mankind as government ambassadors. We choreograph Broadway plays; we produce music that is desired all over the world. We are congressmen, Mayors, and Astronauts. We are the "Real McCoy," who incidentally is also a Black man.

With all that we have accomplished we still find ourselves in a trap, a trap from which we are willing to sever our pride. This trap is between the ears and however specter it is, we condescend to its hold. The crimes resulting from this trap permeate our homes and impacts like a virus that eradicates the concept of esteem, family and self-respect. An iniquity of this nature is not only hard to punish but it is just as difficult to reverse.

I remember at work once when we had a dinner affair scheduled, a fellow Black manager who had just move up the ranks asked me the correct protocol to display at the function. I did not thank anything about it until he asked a question I would never forget. He asked if he should bring his wife or should he bring his white girlfriend. There is was, the trap sprung. At that dinner I observed all say for one lady; all the other women were white. Not all the men were white. I proudly brought my Black lady guest.

Not only did that other Black manager chose to bring his white girlfriend but there were three other Black and two Hispanic managers who chose white companions.

This is malicious malfeasance committed against the spirit, the esteem, and the future of the Black community. This is far more life threatening than drive-by shootings. This sacrilege is drastically more detrimental than selling of or using of drugs. This crime attacks us at our souls. This crime tears at the nucleolus of our self-respect.

From our eminent doctors, lawyers, and businessmen, to our prominent athletes, actors, and performers, prosperity is defined by assimilation. We consummate this assimilation by choosing spouses and mates that resemble our captures. We have contempt for those whom we feel have placed us in the trap, yet we show our contempt by seeking their approval and their acceptance.

Maybe it is I. Possible it's only I who is angered by O.J.'s alleged statement, **"I don't shovel any coal**." Meaning he does not have anything to do with Black women. Maybe I am the only one who heard Michael Jackson state he **"loved"** (past tense), Black when referring to his change of skin color. Is this not like the wolf gnawing at its vital limb?

I hold no animosity, contempt or malice toward my successful Black brothers who chose to select mates outside their own enriched heritage. I'm not sure if I feel hate or hurt every time I find that another of my talented lineage has chosen to free themselves from their perceived trap. I do know I feel deep concern. A deep concern that, in which we are telling our children to hate themselves. Like snipers, we are shooting at them, their mothers, and their fathers with artillery of esteem destroying missiles. Every time a Black man chooses a white woman as a mate, he is telling my young brothers and sisters their mothers are not beautiful. Each time a prominent Black is seen with a white mate, it's viewed as the only way to success is through the infidelity of ones own culture.

Seeing a young life ending from the violence of a drive-by shooting as criminal as it is, happens infinitesimal to the numbers of young lives destroyed by teaching matricide. I'm Black and I'm proud. I love my mother and think she is beautiful. I know I can succeed, not in spite of my color but in regards of my color.

Because of the crimes committed against my Black queens I could not hold any vindictive feelings against the ladies of my desire, I hated and despised my Black Brothers for taking away my ladies away from me. My fury needed to be released, I wanted to strike out and punish someone for my pain. What happened was that I became my own worst malefactor.

In the book, "Great Expectations" by Charles Dickens, There is a girl that is raised by an awful vindictive old lady. The old lady, Miss Halverson, was left at the altar by a man and on that day Miss Halverson stopped living a normal life. The very second she knew her groom was not going to come, Miss Halverson stopped the clocks and asked everyone to leave.

For years, Miss Halverson stayed in that house unchanged from her wedding day. As cobwebs grew on her wedding cake and the house deteriorated, Ms. Halverson sat brooding until she came up with a plan to reap her revenge. She adopted a little girl and being a very rich woman Miss Halverson raised that little girl to be a beautiful and well-desired woman. Miss Halverson raised the girl to have no less than a black hart when it came to men.

As the little girl, Estella, grew she became a very black hearted person when it came to boys and eventually men. She was cruel and teasing. She was so attractive that every man wanted her. Estella, making Miss Halverson proud, had men perusing after her while all the time she intended to hurt them.

There was one boy that Estella knew that she grew up with. Pip, as his name was, turned out to be the only man Estella was kind to, although not at the beginning. As they grew, Estella and Pip became good friends. Never once in the adult years did Estella ever intend to hurt Pip. Pip once confessed his love to Estella and she warned him of black hart.

My self-pity and resentment drove me to be very much like Miss Halverson. My hart became darken to the thought of women. I wanted to reap revenge on the fairer sex. I transformed myself into Estella. My soul purpose was to get gratification out of vengefully attacking women. If a dog is what they wanted, then a dog I was going to be. This was not a part of my life I am proud of, but it is true.

Like Estella, I too had my Pip. Pips to me were my Black ladies. I could not find it in what little of a hart I had left to focus my seek and destroy mission on my Black queens. They had enough of a hard time as it was. I went after white women.

White women epitomized to me the cause of my suffering. White women were kept as queens while my Black ladies were treated as bed warmers during slavery. Blond hair a blue eyes are the archetypes of beauty, while all the time they try to look like my Nubian queens, by tanning, having lip injections, and butt implants. White women being herald, as some kind of goddess was the cause of the self-loathing and low esteem of my Black ladies. My blind anger for revenge led down this path.

A white woman was first to be chosen as a viable Vice Presidential candidate, where as a Black man still had not been chosen to that point. The first non-white man to go up in the space shuttle was a white woman not a Black man. Something as minor as the fact that only white hands have been seen tickling the belly of the doughboy caused great anger in me. I thought that we were being taught to hate ourselves.

With all this negative insight feeding my bitter loneliness, I went out to inflict my vengeance on white women. I became Estella. I made myself only available to white women. I offered them a false sense of togetherness as I used them for sex. I offered them nothing, gave them even less as I used them for my bed warmers. Like Estella, I turned my black hart into a weapon to use on women.

I vindicated my actions by thinking the white women were only interested in me for sex too. I thought they looked at me as a big strapping well endowed black buck. It was not until I started to contemplate that thought I began to feel I was not fulfilling my vengeance. I was instead fulfilling their perverted sexual fantasies. I had become the slave that was brought to the woman's room late at night when the master was away.

My thinking all during that time was demented to say the lease. The disturbing truth was I had turned into the very person I hated. I was seen only with white women. I can imagine what went through the minds of the Black ladies that saw me out with these ladies. My sister has a saying when she sees a Black man with a white woman, **"Another Sister saved."**

I have added an ending to my sisters saying. Another Sister saved and another Black mother insulted. I had to put an end to my so-called vengeance. Thank goodness, that period only lasted a short time. Whom I might have hurt, I do not know. In the end, I was the one who was damaged by the whole incident.

REFLECTIONS
LOVE IN BLACK AND WHITE

Why is it we feel the need to look to the other races for companionship? Just what is it they can offer us that a union of two who share the same life experiences can't offer one another.

He says, "Man our women are too hard to live with. They complain about how I look, how I dress, how much money I make, they complain about the car I drive, and man they even complain about how I make love. There is just no pleasing the bitches."

She says, "Our men are doing nothing and going nowhere. All they want is to go out with their buddies. We women have to go out and get jobs in order to feed the children we were dumb enough to have by these bums. The only thing that motivates these ass holes is that little toy they have in their pants."

His reply to her complaints, "Awe man, how can I be anything, the white man keeps me down. He won't let me get anywhere. I'm tired of working for Charley. I am going to do my own thing. I don't need some bossy bitch telling me what to do. All she has to do is what I tell her to do."

Her replay, "I am tired of coming home to a dunking bum who has done nothing all day but scamming while working from job to job. Then he takes my little money and goes out chasing with his friends, and he wants **me!** To jump into bed at his command just for his own gratification, oh no not me!"

He states, "White women know how to treat a man. They never complain about anything. They accept us for what we are. Man there is no loving like a white woman!"

She states, "White men appreciate us. They treat us nice and we do not have to put up with a sex-crazed beast. They do not have misdirected dreams. Besides there are not many good black men out there anyway. Most of our men are in jail or on their way."

He fails to see that the Black lady expects greatness form her Black man, therefore she is relentless at her persistence to motivate her man. The white woman however expects nothing of a black man but sexual puissance.

She fails to see the truth in his story of white tyranny maintaining his ridicule. The white man, feeling threaten by the strength and creativity of the Black man, needs to castrate our men anyway he can, even to use our women in the work place, giving them jobs over our men, or by taking our women away from us. Our men feel as they were less than our women were, and our women are propelled into a position of potency.

I say, "Wake the hell up! We, working together can build a bond that is much more powerful than any other is. As long as our men feel less than our women do, and our women maintain authority over our men, we will never reach mutual equality. We know whom is to win if we continue detach.

I want no lady who is less than I, nor will I allow myself to be less than her."

CHAPTER SIX
STRIKE THREE

It is usually perceived that the search for love is a lady's emotion. Men don't have the same feelings as women therefore men generally are not seeking love in the same manner. This belief is as absurd as believing women do not like sex, and that only men want sex all the time.

I'm not ashamed to admit my feelings. One thing I always teach is how to discard your ego. It is not weak to be a man with emotional needs. Many times ego gets in the way of a man expressing what he feels. I believe that it is much easier to build a wall than to brake down a wall. I always say that I feel sorry for the person that sends me to the lumberyard to buy my first brick.

I say all this only to disclaim the feeling out there that women only, have a hard time finding a mate. Many men like me have just as much a difficult time as many women have in finding a good mate. Only because most men allow their egos to camouflage their true feelings women do not know how hurt we get or how lonely we get.

The saving grace for me is in the memory I have of the loves in my past that got away for one reason or another. I tend to be opposed to memories that were negative. I enjoy remembering the constructive and loving parts of past relationships. Most think life is a learning experience and we learn from our mistakes. I like to look at life as just an experience. If I had to learn something from every encounter or every moment, it would be easy to carry baggage.

Baggage comes from learning what not to do the next time. I have a friend that once told me she knew how to be a good wife. When I questioned why she was divorced, she told me she learned from the past marriage what not to do in the next. It sounds to me she lost the point. What would have happened if she put down her notebook and stop writing down what not to do, and instead just experienced and developed, would she not still be married?

If she opens that notebook in her next marriage, will she not be comparing the next husband to the last? Aren't these two men different people? What about how much she changed between the marriages her notes will be outdated. I want to experience life not take notes. I want to see each new person as a completely different and unique situation.

Just like remembering the sweet aroma of the rose. I didn't take notes on the experience, I just seized the moment. I don't write down what the sunset looks like because each sunset is different. It's because I remember to sweet aroma of the rose, I continue to take a wife. It is because I remember the beauty of the sunset; I chose to see it again and again.

If I took notes I might write down the rose has thorns that pricks your finger, and when that happens you bleed and it hurts. Maybe the next time I see a rose I will avoid it all together, or at best become too cautious when I approach. If I took notes on the sunset I might write that it hurt my eyes to look at the sun, or that the sky reminded me of blood. I might decide to avoid sundowns completely after that and miss out on the splendor of the next.

My search for love is not based on the experiences I wrote down to use in the next situation. Like the aroma of the rose and the splendor of the sunset, I remember the ecstasy of past relationships so much so that I want to find it again. I remember Laura my high school sweetheart. She was my first love and the first to show me how to feel so good inside. I remember Tina the first lady to show me how to discard the restriction life imprisons us with in order to live life to the fullest.

I will forever remember Yvonne, the first lady to show me love unconditionally. Yvonne is the one I regret not marrying. Lastly, I will never forget Megan; she is the one that showed me I could be loved. I spent five wonderful years with her. I just could never get past the fact she was not Black.

Because of these four ladies, I will never give up looking for that feeling of complete paradise. I don't carry with me the memories of the bad moments we spent. More so I chose to never forget the love, passion, friendship, and wonder I felt with these ladies. This I do only to remember why I continue to search.

Feeling the Personal ads had not produced the outcome I hoped for; I decided to try a cyber connection. My sister being a computer whiz introduced me to the life of cyber dating through the computer and the information super highway. That is where I met Latisha.

I had chatted with many ladies and did not get a strong feeling until I met Latisha on line. Latisha and I had a special love in common. We both loved brainteasers. Whenever we connected on line, we would exchange brainteasers. She would leave them on my e-mail. It was a natural way for me to communicate because I spend hours on my computer anyway. The added interest of going on line and talking to Latisha was a pulse as well as a diversion to my work.

Latisha and I communicated for over a month before we decided to talk in person. I was a little gun shy about meeting anyone. The most interesting aspect to meeting Latisha was that we had quite a number of things in common. Latisha felt the same as I in regards to the moral convictions of everyone around us. This more than anything was what made me interested in talking to her with the hope of meeting.

In talking to Latisha on the phone, I found that she was five years younger than I was. This was new for me since until then I had never dated anyone so young. The youngest I ever dated was only a year younger. She also was a bit nervous about meeting me as well, though she never stated so. We talked on the phone for weeks before the proposition of meeting ever came up. During those weeks, the same was true as when we were communicating on the computer. Everyday she would leave me a brainteaser or a joke. I would reciprocate and do the same.

As a person who hates to talk on the phone, it was easy to talk to Latisha. What is even worse is to talk on the phone and have no one speaking. The awkward pauses of listening to air were as dumb to me as buying a toaster and not eating toast. With Latisha, we had many moments where we listened to air and I did not find myself dreading it. If we talked an hour, twenty minuets of which was in quiet. To me the pauses were as if we were sitting together and just holding each other.

When the time came for us to meet, I was a bit excited and hopeful. Latisha and I had hit it off so well on the phone. We were what seemed to be cut from the same mold. She had no children and had not been married. Latisha was looking for the same in a man. We both had old fashion believes and were strong in our convictions. She was a solid member of her church and had the same compassion about her heritage. She believed that being Black was first and foremost, and living as an example for others was paramount.

When I arrived at the restaurant we agreed to meet at for lunch, I first thought to wait in my car to see when she came up. I wanted to see her first before she saw me. Latisha wasn't too descriptive about what she looked like or what she was going to wear. She just told me to be on the look out for a lady in a hat. As I sat in my car looking at the restaurant, the only lady I saw wearing a hat was what appeared to be a retarded lady in a baseball cap.

I thought to myself just my luck to have made a date with a retarded lady, I was ready to leave. This strange lady in the baseball cap was looking around as if she was looking for someone. Thinking that this couldn't be her I decided to go on up to the restaurant and wait. This lady was sitting in the same place Latisha said she would be sitting but I refused to believe this was she. I looked inside the restaurant and out into the parking lot, all the time keeping my eyes away from that lady.

After fifteen minuets passed and Latisha had not showed so, I thought, I decided to ask the strange lady if she was she. I first sat down at the bench. The lady smiled at me as if she was glad I sat next to her, but still I did not say anything. I still had a hard time believing this was the lady I had developed a strong feeling for on the phone. Finally, from out of my gut I asked if she was Latisha. The lady started giggling and blushing. She looked at me and turned away in a blush.

Feeling too through I started to get up and leave when the lady handed me a note. The note had a message of greeting; it also had some clues written on it. The strange lady had gotten up and disappeared while I was reading the note. The note was from Latisha I saw her take off but didn't see where she went. The restaurant was full at the time.

A bit embarrassed that I had been seen talking to the strange lady, but more relieved that she wasn't Latisha; I walked out into the parking lot to figure out the clues. I have to admit, I was very amused by the trick Latisha played on me. Just like the brainteasers, we had been trading each other; she pulled of the ultimate brainteaser.

The first clue was along the lines of what was opposite of front door. I was thinking that was to mean that Latisha somehow was waiting for me at the back door to the restaurant, so I went to the back door to see. She was not there. The second clue was something about a game children play in grammar school, _____ ball.

Feeling the second clue was to mean Latisha was sitting in a Dodge in the parking lot at the back door I went to see if there were and Dodge's out there. The third clue did not make sense to me at first until I came upon a license plate on a Dodge van that matched the clue. When I went up to the van a lady jumped out of the van and gave me another note.

Now I was feeling like a complete idiot. How many people were in on this ruse? How many people were watching me run around the restaurant and parking lot like a confused baboon and laughing at me. I thought that if the second note was more of the same, I was going to get into my car and leave. The second note was simply put to meet Latisha back at the front door.

When I got back to the front door, there was Latisha smiling at me. When I finally realized this was Latisha, the first thing I wanted to do was put her across my knees and spank her for the embarrassment I felt. Instead, we had a good laugh about the whole matter and went in to have lunch.

Latisha was a small little lady. She wore cloths that covered her up completely. My first impression of her was that of a simple church girl. Latisha was not a drop dead gorgeous doll, but she was not a homely ugly rat either. She seemed to be the bashful type. All throughout lunch, she didn't look me in the eyes much. I thought she was just right for me. I was tired of the cutesy type of ladies and the worldly type. Latisha appeared to be the down-home kind of lady, the kind you bring home to mother.

After lunch, Latisha and I went our separate ways. I was pleased and honored the have met her. Over the next seven months, we made time to see each other and talked every day. Latisha had to me strange hours at work. She would work different shifts around the clock. We spent a lot of time talking on the phone. Much of the time spent on the phone was in silence. I could not believe how much I enjoyed saying nothing to her on the phone. Like I said, it was as if we were cuddled up and enjoying the moment.

When Latisha and I got together, I had never felt an enjoyment felt with any other lady. It was as if I was spending the day with myself because we were so much alike. We enjoyed the same simple things in life. She was very much involved with her family and would involve me. One thing the Latisha would constantly repeat was that I was too good to be true.

When I first met her mother, it was at a family Bar-B-Q at her grandmother's house. Latisha asked me to come over and have supper. I was flattered to meet her family. She gave me directions to her Grandmothers house and I was to meet her there.

When I arrived, Latisha ran up to me, threw her arms around me, and gave me a huge hug. Her hug surprised me and made me feel extremely special at the same time.

Latisha and I had been seeing each other for weeks before this Bar-B-Q. For some reason I didn't feel Latisha had many men in her life before me. In other words, I thought she was a virgin. Feeling proud of that fact, without ever asking, I chose not to approach her in the same manner I might have if I thought she was not a virgin. I had never kissed her or even thought about anything other than that. When she hugged me at her Grandmother's house, I was in second heaven.

When Latishas' mother came into the room, I recognized her as the lady in the Dodge van. I also recognized at the Bar-B-Q the retarded lady that was at the restaurant. Latisha's mother was just a sweet as Latisha. She was an attractive lady that made me happy just incase Latisha and I were to get serious I knew she would grow old lovely. I met her whole family at the Bar-B-Q.

As the Bar-B-Q was dying down, Latisha's mother along with others were playing cards. They invited me to join in. I had not played cards in over fifteen years but it all came back to me soon as I started to play. These people were serious about their card playing. They liked to play the game, Spades, and could play all night and well into the morning.

It was about one o'clock in the morning when they decided to go to Latisha's mothers' house to finish playing cards. At Latisha's mom's house, I understood why Latisha had such strange hours at work. It turned out that she was a police officer. There was a picture of her in uniform sitting on a mantle place. I had a feeling that was what she was from the background noises I herd when she called from work. I couldn't see her as a cop. She was too small and petite. Around four o'clock in the morning I was too tired to continue playing cards.

That evening was an example of the many great times we spent together. nothing fancy, just enjoying family and friends. I was beginning to fall in love with this lady. Once we played one on one basketball with each other. That was the first time I realized Latisha was a very well put together lady. She was wearing shorts and a tee shirt. She was indeed small, but all mussel. She still was very much a lady still.

I remember the day I knew I wanted to have Latisha in my life forever. One day coming home from work, I had an accident on the freeway. My car blew a rear tire and flipped over during rush hour. The odd thing was that I not only survived the accident, the car landed back on its tires and out of harms way without hitting another car. When things settled down in my mind, the radio was tuned to a religious station of which I was not tuned to.

When I got home, I called my mother to tell her what had happened and to let her know I was all right. Just after I hung up the phone with my mother, Latisha called. She asked if I were all right. She sounded as if she knew I was in trouble. I informed her of what had happened. Latisha then told me she was in her squad car and had a bad feeling about me. When I asked her what time she had that feeling, she told me the time. Ironically, the time she gave was the exact same time I was in the accident.

It was as if our souls were connected. Latisha also told me at that time she had never feared her job until she met me. She had known from the beginning she wanted to be a police officer. She had always did her job well but never considered the dangers. Once meeting me, she began to consider the dangers. She said I was too good to be true. I was what she always wanted.

That is when I felt this was the lady I was going to spend my life with. At that point, we had been seeing each other for over five months. We had known each other for a year if you count the time we communicated on computer and phone prior to meeting. I was feeling spiritually connected to Latisha.

The night I knew I was in love with Latisha was the night we spent together. I had told Latisha early on in our relationship that I liked pizzas and that I would marry to first lady that could make my favorite pie, lemon meringue. Latisha invited me over to make pizzas this day. We had fun coming up with all kinds of creations. Later in the day, Latisha pulled out a lemon meringue pie she made. She had called her mother at lease five times to make sure she got it right. I was impressed, and it did taste good.

That night we were sitting on a comfort chair listing to the radio. We were just coddled up and enjoying each others company. Both of us fell asleep holding each other. That night we never got up we just sat there cuddled up and keeping each other warm. That to me was a most enjoyable night. One I will never forget. That is when I knew I loved Latisha.

For seven months of being with Latisha or the year and a half of knowing her was a happy time in my life. I hoped it would always be like that. Unfortunately my luck would not let my happiness last. The one constant phrase the Latisha always muttered played an important part of my sorrow. I was too good to be true.

One week it was apparent Latishas phone calls were not as frequent as before. When I called her and leave a message on the answering machine, she would take a day to return my calls. Before when I called, she would call back within hours. I felt there was something wrong but when asked, Latisha would say nothing was wrong.

Soon it took days for Latisha to return my calls. Then it took weeks. I tried not to force anything so I would accept this from her not knowing what was wrong. She would tell me what the problem was. Weeks then turned into months for Latisha to return my calls. By now, I was not even able to see her. Still I did not want to force the issue. I felt she had something to work out.

I had called my sister for advice. She told me that it was possible that everything was moving too fast for Latisha and that she needed to work through some demons. My sister told me to give it time. From what I told my sister of my relationship with Latisha, she thought maybe Latisha wanted space to find herself. So I gave Latisha the space.

Four months passed before I herd from Latisha again. It was disturbing to hear her act as if nothing had happened. She tried to carry on a conversation as if we had been in communication all the time. I decided to put an end to the thought of giving her space. I asked Latisha to tell me what happened to us. At first, she would not admit to any problem. When I told her I could not take it any more, she decided to confess.

Once again, she told me I was too good to be true. Latisha told me of the women she runs into on calls at work who have been battered by their mates. Latisha told me of her father who has been nothing but a disappointment her entire life. She told me of her brother who is in and out of jail for nasty reasons. She told me that men have proven to be bad forces in her life. I was too good to be true, she was waiting for the other shoe to drop, and I would show my true colors.

Not knowing how to respond to her, I told her there are no guarantees in life. I had no plans of mistreating her and that if I were in fact too good to be true, why not at lease enjoy it until something goes wrong, at lease then she would have reason to disappear on me. I could tell I was not getting through. She agreed not to be so distant, but once off the phone she continued in the same manner.

In time, I would only get a call from Latisha out of the blue. She would act as if we had never stopped talking. Another year would pass with Latisha calling so sporadically. Once I tried to put my foot down and begged her to stop holding me at length. When that didn't work, I finally told her not to call anymore because she was hurting me by calling and staying distant.

REFLECTIONS
THE REWARD OF
SINCERITY

I was sincere in love. I was honest, devoted, and I invested all of my time and energy to make the union work. You in spite of my favor saw me as feeble and weak. What breed of man is kind, honest, and devoted, unless he is week, you would state just prior to letting me go.

Why is it you complain they you cannot ever find a man. You always say, "All the good ones are married". You declare you want a man who is sensitive, caring, and honest, a man who can show his true feelings. When I come along, you cannot deal with my sincerity, and you leave me all alone.

I often wonder what it is you truly want. I see you with men that beat you, lie to you, cheat on you, and you never leave, yet My reward for sincerity is loneliness and pain.

CHAPTER SEVEN
THE GREEN GOWN

After having such a bad luck in romance I had to evaluate why I was having such problems. I had no choice but to start to take a good look at the man in the mirror. It had to be me that was the problem. First, I evaluated my divine belief that I might find nirvana in a relationship. The evidence speaks for itself. I cannot honestly find one friend or coworkers that could claim they are happy in their marriage. For that matter, I cannot pinpoint witnessing a happy marriage at all in my life. Every married man I know was cheating on his wife. I even knew men who were cheating on their wives by seeing other men. Nirvana cannot exist in this sick world.

In the teachings of Buddha, it is written:

> *"Because of their ignorance, all people are always thinking wrong thoughts and always losing the right viewpoint and clinging to their egos, they take wrong actions. As a result, they become attached to a delusive existence."*

I had obviously lost to correct viewpoint. By looking for a perfect person, I had limited my options. By seeking a prefect relationship, I was enacting an ego that believes in fairytales. I had to realize that in relationships people carry a lot of baggage, baggage of past traumas, of insecurities, of concealment, and deceit that is used for protection. I too carry this baggage.

I opened the baggage of mine to see the bones I bore. I had then to look at my attitude. Brenda I feared because I was insecure of myself. I feared I couldn't hold on to her. Valerie I discounted because of greed. I was afraid of loosing the spoils I had attained. Patrice I lost due to my lack of straightforwardness. Had I confronted her up front rather than playing the sleuth game, things might have resulted differently. Obviously, my protection guards were up. Obviously, my fears were evoked.

"He who covers his sins will not prosper, but whoever confesses and forsakes them will have mercy."

—Proverbs 28:13

Looking inward at myself proved to show a man who wanted a relationship so bad, who wanted to defy the odds and have a relationship that was perfect. Who was foolish to expect so much yet give so little? I had put up too many walls to protect myself. I was determined that the next time I wasn't going to allow myself to be so guarded. I was going to let loose and drop my stuffiness. I was going to stretch out and grab for the golden ring.

One day at work a customer I had helped came back and handed me her business card. On the back was her home phone number. To me she was just a customer. While I was helping her, I never considered anything more than that. After getting her card, I stopped to take a second look. What I saw was exciting.

Her name was Janet and from the front of her business card, she was a vice president of a one of the Black organizations in Los Angeles. She had classic Nubian looks. She also had a classic Nubian physique. To be more direct Baby Had Back! Moreover, plenty of it. It's a wonder I didn't notice while I was helping her. Right away, my first thought was that this was a customer. I couldn't date a customer! Then I remembered my new decree not to limit myself. Drop the guards my man and go for the golden ring.

I called Janet that night. It turned out that she had never been married but did have a daughter nineteen years old. Janet Had only had been in Los Angeles three years. Her daughter was in Texas where they were from. Her job offered a transfer that she couldn't refuse. The chance to come to Los Angeles was a dream of hers, a dream she wished now hadn't come true.

For the first hour on the phone, Janet and I talked about the differences between the east coast and the west coast. We talked about how bad it was to live in a Los Angeles, which was worse for Black people than the south, when it came to racism. How the city of angles are full of tempting devils. How Blacks try too hard to separate themselves from the community. To be Black anywhere in this country was a challenge no matter what state, only in L.A. one is lulled into believe things are different and they are not.

We hit it off so well on the phone that we decided to meet. Janet was going to be in a community play sponsored by her church and invited me to come. After the play, we could get together and see what was going to happen next. She left a ticket for me at the door. The play was at a predominately-Black high school.

The theme of the play was anti drug use. It was a musical. Janet had a little part in it. She played a rapping drugged out prostitute. It was funny in areas and sad in others. It was easy to see the players were not professional actors but they carried it off very well. It was a good play. One of the most enlightening events that occurred that night did not happen on stage, it was in the audience. Not one of the men brought white women. I saw what appeared to be successful Black men there with Black ladies. I saw Black families in tact. This was the first time I had experience this type of unity the eight years I had lived in L.A. to that point.

After the play, I waited for Janet to come out to meet me. I waited for what seemed like forever. One lady there kept staring at me and smiling. She made me a bit uncomfortable because everywhere I would go to get away from her, she would follow. Finally, I asked if I could help her. She winked at me and asked if I was with anyone. When I told her I was, and started to walk away, she started laughing uncontrollable. She grabbed my arm, reached up, and removed a wig. It was Janet; she still had on her wig from the play.

She had wondered if I would remember what she looked like, so she came up with a way to trick me and it worked. I have to admit I didn't really get a good look at her in my office and thought I might not know what she was going to look like. I was not expecting her to do that to me. When I saw her on stage the only way I knew it was her was because she told me what part she was going to play. Even at that, she was so well draped in clothes on stage I could not make her out.

Janet escorted me back stage laughing all the way to wait for her to get all her things together. We decided to meet at a restaurant down the street and left in separate cars. At the restaurant, I finally got to get a good look at her. She had medium length hair that she wore in curls. As I said before, she had a classic Nubian features. Her face was narrow with a full mouth that when broke into a smile would melt you like butter. She had a little peach fuss atop her upper lip that somehow made her even sexier.

Janet's body was a masterpiece. Not one ounce of fat on her. She had big thighs and a narrow waist, but she had this butt. Oh boy did she have a butt! Janet was wearing a peach dress that fitted her just write. Peach just happens to be my favorite color on Black women. I think Peach makes My Black lady look extremely sexy. Janet wore the hell out of that peach dress. In addition, that butt! Janet wore a chain belt around her waist the one end fell just above her area that dreams are made of.

We had a salad bar for dinner and I couldn't wait for her to get back up so I could see her walk away. Lord have mercy! To be honest I don't remember much about what we talked about at dinner. All I remember was that Janet had the voice of an angle with her cute faint southern accent. She had the eyes of a goddess. She had the body of a nymph, and that butt! All else about dinner didn't matter.

We must have hit it off very well at dinner because neither of us wanted the night to end so soon. We decided to take her car home and we would go to the beach. We walked along the pier until we came upon a karaoke club. We went in to watch the show, and during the show, Janet got up and sang. Janet sang a love song to me. I was really flattered that she would have the nerve to do such a thing. I could never do that. The people in the next booth turned to me and stated that she must really love me. I was even more flattered. They didn't know we were on our first date yet they could see the love that was blooming.

Janet had a voice of an angle and when she sang, the sweetness of her voice became even more apparent. I enjoyed watching her strutting across the floor singing that song. Every time she came over to me and looked into my eyes and that lovely song danced across those luscious lips, I would melt. I was not a believer in love at first sight, but I was beginning to believe in love at first song. My emotions for Janet were multiplying by the seconds.

After leaving the bar, Janet and I walked along the beach until we came upon a little kid's park. I asked her to join me on the swings and she told me that she loved to swing. Watching that peach dress slither in the wind of Janet's swinging looked like my angle sprouted wings. We swung on the swings until our peace was compromised by another couple. We both had to work the next day so we decided to call it a night. When I took her home, I wasn't going to do as I have always done before and not kiss goodnight even if I knew the lady wanted a kiss. I wanted Janet to know I enjoyed her company and wasn't about to place any doubt. I kissed her very passionately and said goodnight.

The next day when we talked on the phone I had to try to get to know Janet. The previous night was like a dream and I remembered nothing of any conversation we might have had. I found out that Janet was from Texas and had only been in L.A. for three years. She told me she was living with her cousin and that he was always gone because he was in the military. She told me her daughter was still in Texas because she had four children to care for. She said her daughter was coming to L.A. once Janet fond her own place to live. Janet stated she missed her grand babies.

My first flag was raised. Janet had her baby at sixteen years old herself. She left her child when the child was sixteen. That had to be true if her daughter was nineteen and Janet was in L.A. three years. Now she tells me that she is a grandmother of four babies from a child that is only nineteen. Something just didn't seem right about that picture. Remembering my commitment to myself not to let judgmental baggage in get in my way, I ignored the flag, and said nothing.

As soon as that flag was raised, Janet raised another. She told me she shared her apartment with her cousin's roommate. This roommate was a man. The roommate was a recruiter for the service and had an office near their apartment. He only stayed there when he did not feel like driving the hour and a half to his real home where his wife and children lived. Janet asked if I might have a problem with that because she hoped I would not.

My baggage of ego busted open. The bones were telling me not to go any further with this. I politely packed them up and through them away because I was not going to allow myself to loose out on a good thing by being so cautious. I told Janet I would have a problem with it if she had not told me first, which was a lie, but if she told me, there was nothing going on between the two of them I would not worry. The rest of the conversation that night went without any more flags, which I was glad about. We talked about the previous night and how we both felt something, we never felt before.

That night when I went to bed I forced myself to ignore the flags. I wanted only to think of Janet in the way I felt about her the night before. I was proud of myself for not giving up too easy. I felt this time I was going to find just what I wanted. Janet had not shown she was a bad person so why should I feel likewise. I was finally able to go to sleep with anticipation of our next meeting.

The next time we got together, I took Janet to an African Marketplace by my house. The marketplace was held the first Saturday of every month. I thought she might get a kick out of going to it. Many of the booths had artwork and trinkets. Two of the booths had clothes and cloths from Africa. Janet fell in love with one outfit that she wanted me to take her to the bank so she could buy it. When we got to my place, she modeled it for me. If she had Nubian features before, she surely had them after adorning herself with clothes from the motherland. She was a knock out.

I told her she looked like a beautiful queen of the Nile. Her beauty was powerful enough to lay aside the waters of the great Nile so that she could cross it. I meant every word of it. If there was ever anybody that belonged in the clothes of our motherland, it was Janet. Many of us wear Kente Cloth and do not do it justice. Janet's wearing of Kente Cloth to me embodied the meaning of homeland. From that moment on, Janet always bought some form of African wear whenever she shopped.

The night I first made love to Janet was unforgettable. She called me at work to see what time I was getting off. When she found I was not getting out until very late she asked me to come over. I told her it would be too late for me to get there. Janet asked that I come anyway because she had something to tell me. Thinking something was wrong, thinking she was about to tell me to take a long walk on a short pier, I hurried over to get the bad news. If this dream was going to come to an end, so be it.

When Janet let me into the apartment, she had a very serious expression. She started by telling me how much she enjoyed spending time with me. I began to think this was the; >It's not you it's me,' speech, so I listened on with dread. She went on to tell of how good I was to her and how much she appreciated me introducing her to her African heritage. I'm now thinking this is going to be the; >you're too good for me,' speech.

Then Janet said something that blew me away. "I love you." I had not been prepared for that. When she said it, I felt relieved on one hand and frighten on the other hand. We had only known each other for a month and a half. My flags started waving violently. My baggage of mistrust, fear, and sanctuary all unzipped at once. How could I trust what she just said with us only knowing each other for only a short time? I was afraid that we were moving too fast. I thought I should tell her to slow down because it was too soon, but I knew this would have been an act of safety. I would have been seeking sanctuary for my feelings. I caught a hold of that baggage and through them out the window as I had the others.

When Janet was able to regain my attention, she asked if I herd her. I told her I did and did not expect it. Janet repeated it again. She told me she had felt it from the first but did not want to acknowledge it. Once she decided to acknowledge it, she needed the right time to tell me and this was that right time. What became typical of Janet was about to happen this time as it had before. When she caused one flag to be waived and I disregarded, she caused another.

Janet felt the need to be completely honest with me now that she had fallen in love with me and trusted the feeling to be true. At first, I thought of the room-mate. I had seen many women spending the night with him. I asked Janet on many occasions why she put up with a man that was married living in her apartment and using it to cheat on his wife. She would tell me that the apartment belonged to her cousin and she didn't have enough money to move out on her own. Therefore, I thought she was going to tell me that she had been involved with him.

Janet instead laid a much heavier bomb on me. She told me that the apartment belonged to her ex boyfriend. She told me of how she really moved from

Texas because she had just met a man who was in the service and about to be stationed in San Diego. She decided to follow him to San Diego where they made a life for themselves until after two years he was transferred to L.A. where she now lived.

She went on to tell me that once they moved into that apartment, she found out he had impregnated a Hispanic girl down the street. After finding this out she nearly went crazy because she had given up so much to be with him. She had left her family, her daughter and her grand babies, and this was how he rewarded her. Still she couldn't find it in herself to leave because she loved him so much. Once she forgave him, it didn't take him much time to tell her he was moving out to live with a white woman he met.

This time she did go crazy. Janet told me she had a nervous brake down. She had to check herself into a clinic for a while. Once back on her feet she refused to allow him to take advantage of her. She said that is why she stayed in that apartment. He owed her that if nothing else. She wanted him to pay until she was able to get back on her feet. She also told me the car she drove was in his name. She told me the reason she was telling me now was to clear the air. She offered that if I wanted to call it quits I could and she would understand.

At the end of that confession a slew of baggage unveiled, far too many to name. Flags were waving and horns were blowing. I had to force myself to remember my conviction that there wasn't a perfect relationship. OK, I told myself this isn't what you wanted to hear, but it's not something you can't get over. I fought the bones back into their concealment but this time I did not discard them. Somehow, I would have preferred her to tell me it was the roommate. I told Janet I did not want to leave, that my feeling for her were just as strong for her as hers for me.

She thanked me for understanding and asked me to stay the night. I did not understand but I wanted to. I followed Janet into the bedroom and was floored by yet one more interference. On her nightstand was a book entitled, **"How to Win Him Back From That Other Woman."** When I saw the book, I asked her why she had it. She told me she bought it while she was in the hospital recovering from her breakdown; she never tossed it out once she was over him.

Janet wanted me to make love to her that night. As hard as I tried, the best I could do was a feeble attempt. The thought that I was in another man's bed, in another man's apartment along with the story she gave, compounded with that book staring me in my mind, I was too frustrated and bothered to perform well. In fact, from that time on I could not perform well at her apartment period.

When I made love to Janet at my place, it was only a little better. For as long as she stayed under the purse strings of this man, I felt inhibited. I never told this to Janet I just tried to fight back the feelings and tried to please her.

After a few weeks thing were back to normal. I tried my best to only make love to Janet at my place when ever possible. She would reinforce time and time again that she loved me. Once I was at one of my favorite African stores. The owner had just got in a new line of clothes from Kenya. There was one outfit that was of supreme quality. When he showed it to me, I knew it would be perfect for Janet. I had bought tickets to see Robert Townsend's stage adaptation of his film **"The Five hart Beats."** I thought this would be the best time to spring it on her.

When I sprang it on her she was like a child in a candy store, she loved it. She immediately put it on instead of what she was going to wear to the play. She looked great, so much so that at the play all heads turned as we came in. The other ladies wearing their tight body hugging outfits, paled by comparison to Janet. We looked like visiting royalty from Africa.

After the Play, we had a late dinner. At the restaurant, quite a few people complimented Janet on her outfit. Many white women that came over asked us if we were visiting from out of town. I felt proud being with such a stunning beautiful Nubian queen. That night Janet spent the night at my place. We lit my fireplace and had wine. She told me she loved me, and I told her I loved her. That was the first time I had ever told any lady I was dating, I loved them. It shocked me when I said it. Needless to say, Janet was finally pleased to hear me finally return her love. That night when I made love to Janet we made the best love of our relationship.

My mom has a habit of talking about her children a work. There are a few ladies in this world that know me better than many of my friends do. When my mom told them about Janet, they said it would not last. They knew I did not date women with children. They knew about Janet's daughter but did not know about the grandchildren or of the other problems, I had to overcome. When they heard I was still with Janet after so long, one of the ladies told my mother I was going to marry this one. When my mom told me this, I just laughed. Little did they know that was far from the truth!

Janet and I had talked about getting married. She offered to make a run to Vegas to have a quickie wedding. We had begun to redecorate my house for when the time came. I resisted a quickie wedding because I still had that baggage I hadn't thrown away. I felt it necessary for Janet to get out from under that ex's protection before I could feel right in us starting something. I told her I will marry her after that happened.

For Janet's birthday, I wanted to do something really special. I told her I would pick her up at work and we would go out to dinner. Earlier in the day, I had a dozen roses sent. She was shocked when the limo driver went in with another dozen roses to escort her to the car. Her whole staff followed her out. She was in tears of joy as she said good-by to them. We had dinner off the ocean and later took a midnight harbor cruise.

Janet told me no man had ever treated her as I had. She told me about a man back in Texas that she lived with that beat her and forced her to sell drugs for him. She told me of a man that brutally raped her and left her for dead. She told me of a man that her daughter told Janet molested her. She said she did not believe her daughter and sent her daughter to live with her mother. That man ended up in the streets whacked out on drugs. Janet told me that until I came along, she never believe love could be expressed in such a nice feeling way. She told me she did not deserve me.

As time grew closer for Janet's lease to end on that apartment, my greatest fears came true. Earlier in our relationship, as a matter of fact the night of our first date, I had a dream that Janet and I were at a dinner party. She had on a long flowing form-fitting gown. At the dinner party, Janet was ignoring me and flirting with every man in the place. I got tired of her behavior and left her there. I never saw her again after that.

Now that was just a dream. I have a history however, of never dreaming about people I know. When I do, the dream usually comes true. This was just one more baggage I did not toss aside either. I never told Janet about the dream; I just went on not letting it affect our relationship. I did however find a chance to search through Janet's closet one day to see if she owned such a dress. I told her I wanted to see how much closet space I would need when we got married. She did not own such a dress and I was glade to see that.

Ironically, Janet's job was throwing a big party. Janet wanted me to go with her to pick out the dress. We went to a store I knew about. I had been shopping with many women and knew where she might find a very nice evening dress. Janet picked out three dresses to try on. Two were gold and one was green. She tried on the first gold and came out for me to see. It did not fit her good at all. She tried on the second gold dress. It fit all right but didn't really say anything to me.

When she came out with the green dress on, I was floored. She looked delicious. Being an honest sort, I had to tell her I liked the green dress best. I told her this with that dream on my mind, but I couldn't lie. Janet was favoring to the second gold dress. After much debate, she decided to buy the green dress. The flowing form fitting green dress.

The drive home after buying the dress Janet was very quiet. When I asked was something wrong she said nothing. I asked her again what was wrong and she just told me that she did not deserve me. Feeling that was strange I said nothing else and drove her home with that green dress in my car. When I got to her place, she told me not to come in that she had a headache and want to rest. Feeling that was strange I said OK and went home.

Later that night Janet called me crying. She told me she could not see me anymore. Crushed, I asked why she was doing this to us. She told me that her daughter was having another baby and the state wanted to take it away from her, so Janet wanted to go back to Texas and try to make it right by her daughter. She further stated she had known for some time her daughter was going to have a fifth baby out of wedlock, but did not know what to do until then.

I knew there was something more to the story than what Janet was telling me, so I asked if I could come over so we could talk about it. Janet said I could not come over but she would be glade to meet me somewhere. Feeling this was a strange request I told her that if she had already made her mind up then I agreed that she needed to finally be a mother to her daughter.

The day after Janet was supposed to leave for Texas, I called her number. A strange man answered her phone and I knew it was not her roommate. I hung up without saying anything. The next morning I called again. This time Janet answered the Phone. I had my suspicions confirmed. Janet had gone back to her ex. All the signs were there and I chose to ignore them. I wanted to go for the golden ring and instead received the most painful heartache I ever had. I soon learned that one chapter in that book; **"How to Win Him Back from That Other Woman,"** tells of having you ex believe he may loose you for good. Janet used me to get that two timing, low life, back into her life to no doubt hurt her again.

I have never hated someone in my life as much as I hate Janet. To use a man's emotions the way she did, to build up someone's hopes the way she did, only so she could retrieve scum back into her life, I was horrified as to what kind of demon I fell for. To think that the only lady I told, I loved, was such a monster sickened me.

In the teachings of Buddha, it is written:

> *"An insincere and evil friend is more to be feared than a wild beast; a wild beast may wound your body, but an evil friend will wound your mind."*

The pain inflected on me by Janet was so excruciating that I thought I would never get over it, and maybe I have not yet.

> *"Behold, all those who were incensed against you shall be ashamed and disgraced; they shall be as nothing, and those who strive with you shall perish."*

> *"You shall seek them and not find them-those who contended with you. Those who war against you shall be as nothing, as a nonexistent thing."*

> *—Isaiah 41:11-12*

YOU SHOWED ME HOW TO CRY

As a child I never cried, when I was punished
    I never cried
When I would hurt myself
    I never cried
There were times when I would try and force myself
    yet I couldn't cry
My best friend was killed
    yet I couldn't cry
My father died in a work accident
    yet I couldn't cry
I was beginning to think there was something wrong with me
    then I met you
Your love composed feelings I never felt before
    and I cried
There were times you made me feel exceptionally good
    and I cried
There were times you evoked anguish
    and I cried
At times we would cry together
    You showed me how to cry.
You have depart from my life
    I cry no more

The teaching of Buddha state:

> *"To be idle is a short road to death and to be diligent is a way of life; foolish people are idle, wise people are diligent."*

Therefore, I will continue to search...

ABOUT THE AUTHOR

About me, and who am I? I could tell you about my successes in business and education. I could tell you about my failures. I could tell you of all the places I've traveled to and inform you of my worldly treasures. This is not who I am nor is it what I'm about.

I am the people who bravely walked across the ice bridge to populate the world from the great continent of Africa where all life began. I am the Zulu the Masai. I am the men and women who were savagely stolen from their lands and placed into slavery throughout the globe. I am the thousands of men who died fighting for freedom in the civil war whose reward was segregation and lynching. I am the men and women, who lived and died trying to survive in a land they built and were not welcome to stay in.

I am the men who died in World War II fighting the evils of Hitler only to come home to evils of Jim Crow. I am the freedom fighters whose strength was so great that they allowed dogs to bite them and allow fire hoses turned on them to empower the future with civil rights.

I am the convertible top, the traffic light and the multitudes of inventions created by men and women of Africa decent. I am the doctors and lawyers and I am the crack head and the criminal. I am the home owner and the welfare family. I am the strong beautiful single Black mother and I am the drunk and skirt chaser, I am the person running from who I am and I am the proud Black man standing in your face.

I am the child in the ghetto with no hope for future and success and I am the privileged child who is expected to be a success. I am a sum total to all my people. Those who had struggled those who have failed and those who have succeed. I am the sum total of every black man and woman in the past, the present and into the future. What I have is because of them. What I am about is knowing where I came from, what I live with and what I'll have in the future. All my people is who I am!

978-0-595-40351-6
0-595-40351-4